LIVES
An Anthropological Approach
to Biography

CHANDLER & SHARP PUBLICATIONS IN ANTHROPOLOGY
AND RELATED FIELDS

GENERAL EDITORS: L. L. LANGNESS AND ROBERT B. EDGERTON

Lives
An Anthropological Approach to Biography

L. L. LANGNESS
University of California, Los Angeles

GELYA FRANK
University of California, Los Angeles

Chandler & Sharp Publishers, Inc.
Novato, California

Photograph Credits

Front Cover: Edward S. Curtis
Back Cover: Clockwise from the upper right—Sylvia Kennedy,
Douglass R. Price-Williams, Sylvia Kennedy, L. L. Langness

Library of Congress Cataloging in Publication Data

Langness, L. L. (Lewis L.), 1929–
    Lives : an anthropological approach to
biography.

    (Chandler & Sharp publications in anthro-
pology and related fields)
    Bibliography: p.
    Includes index.
    1. Biography. 2. Anthropology—Methodology.
I. Frank, Gelya, 1948–   II. Title.
III. Series.
GN346.6.L36   920   81-15460
ISBN 0-88316-542-2   AACR2

Book design by Joe Roter.
Composition by Marin Typesetters.

Portions of this book appeared earlier in *The Life History in Anthropological Science*, by
L.L. Langness, copyright © 1965 by Holt, Rinehart and Winston.

Contents

Acknowledgments

We are indebted to many friends and colleagues who have given us generous help and encouragement. In particular we are grateful to John G. Kennedy for his insightful comments on the original draft. We also would like to extend special thanks to Hilda Kuper and Barbara G. Myerhoff for comments and help in many extraordinary ways. Many people read portions of the manuscript at various stages in the writing and helped us refine this book through successive drafts. In particular, we wish to thank Joan Cassell, Robert B. Edgerton, Jacki A. Gallagher, Nancy S. Halpern, Mahmood Ibrahim, Dixie Lee King, Joseph J. Kockelmans, Laurie Levin, Charlotte Linde, Betty Macias, Jenine Meltzer, Oreste F. Pucciani, Sharon L. Sabsay, and Jim L. Turner. Betsy Hall shared the burden of editing the manuscript for publication. Lupe Montaño and Crystal Brian provided patient and understanding secretarial assistance when it was most needed. Naturally we are alone responsible for whatever shortcomings may be present.

Note

In writing this book the authors have tried to carry out the 1974 resolution of the American Anthropological Association on the generic use of the term "man." We have therefore avoided gender-specific terms ("men," "man," "mankind") for groups of people and the personification of such groups as male ("the person's view of his life . . ."). We have respected the original language of the works we cite, however, and quotations from these appear intact.

LIVES
An Anthropological Approach
to Biography

Introduction

Lives: An Anthropological Approach to Biography comes out of a movement at this time toward what might be called "person-centered" ethnography. What this consists of is a rigorous yet compassionate effort on the part of American scholars and others to portray the lives of ordinary individuals, in cultures and contexts sometimes far removed from the ones they know, with the kind of perceptiveness and detail that transform a stranger we might meet in our personal lives into a friend. In finding ways to give voice to persons in a range of societies—many of them members of subgroups shuffled about in the continual struggle of class interests and shifting national alliances—anthropologists who use the life-history method convey directly the *reality* that people other than themselves experience. But we do not want to dwell exclusively on the idea that other worlds are miles away or in some enclave—religious, geographical, or ethnic. Getting to know any person in depth is a major experience because we have to admit that another way of structuring the world truly exists. Cultural differences make such alternatives easier to spot, but more difficult to comprehend.

A book on the life history in anthropology—an approach whose wellsprings go back to the 1920s, that has much in common with the biographical methods used in other disciplines and yet offers much to them—should be launched, we feel, by the people whose lives are ultimately our concern. Permit us to present one or two brief portraits.

It is 1937. Helena Valero, an eleven-year-old girl of Spanish descent, is sailing up the Rio Dimiti by canoe with her parents and brothers in the dense tropical jungle between Venezuela and Brazil. A year earlier, she had been studying at a mission school on the Rio Uaupés but her father was asked to take her back home because such schools were made for the Indians, not for "civilized" people. Now the family is going to settle at an isolated place on the Dimití where Helena's uncle has built two small European-style houses and cleared three gardens. As they come nearer to the spot, white smoke drifts toward them in the morning air. Helena's mother suggests: "Perhaps some huntsman is smoking his meat in my brother's empty house." They land and Helena's father goes in the direction of the houses, his machete in hand. The smoke is coming not from there but from the edge of the camp. When her father returns, blood is trickling down his arm where he has been hit with a poisoned arrow.

The family scrambles back into the canoe, throwing all their possessions into the river so they can row faster. A good distance away, all is silent when suddenly arrows pelt them from the bank. Eight arrows strike Helena's father. He pulls them all out. An arrow pins Helena's own thigh to her belly. With effort and in haste, her mother bites the point out with her teeth. Helena recalls: "Then we all threw ourselves into the water; my head was spinning and I couldn't swim, but my mother held me up by the arm. We reached the bank; my father took me in his arms and began to run like a drunken man towards the woods, leaning onto the branches. I remember that all the trees were swimming around my head; my sight was growing misty. I could hear the shouts of the Indians nearby, for they had run towards the canoe. Then I remember only that I said to my father: 'Father, leave me, I'm dying.' " When Helena awakens, it is night and a fire is burning, around which an old man is singing shaman's songs. She is surrounded by Indians, terrifying in their nakedness, men and women alike with lower lips distended by huge plugs of tobacco, speaking a language she cannot understand.

The narrative of Helena Valero, tape-recorded by ethnographer Ettore Biocca (1971) begins here. Captured in rapid succession by enemy tribes of Yanoáma Indians, many times in danger for her life and forced to flee alone into the forest where tenacity and a precocious intelligence kept her alive, taken in marriage by one chief and then another, Valero eventually escaped with the second of these men and her sons after 20 years among these people, years of futile plans and attempts to return to her home. Helena Valero witnessed a way of life in uncharted territory that never before or since had been seen so closely by a European and that today is headed for extinction under the genocidal policies of Amazonian development. This existence and its people were unimaginably fierce—but not entirely so, or at all times. Without reason other than kindness, Valero was fed and protected by certain of her captors, who urged the restraint of violence on her behalf. With some she describes a relationship of love. And she herself came to see things through Yanoáma eyes, enough so that she describes in this way her own ceremonial ornamentation at puberty: hair sheared in a bowl shape and shaved in the middle; body painted red; wavy black lines on legs, chest, back, and face; cotton bands under knees and on feet and around wrists and breasts: "I really looked beautiful."

The Italian ethnographer to whom Valero told her story writes: "It was life in the forest seen from within, seen by men who consider us whites as their eternal enemies, the creators of diseases and of death; it was the hatreds, the sudden acts of generosity, the betrayals, the agreements, the sons of the witch-doctors, the magic practices: It was a world, that is, completely new, which no white man certainly had ever seen, and which Helena Valero revealed to me" (1971:12). Her story confirmed for Biocca that "one makes a grave error if one supposes that the men of the forest are wild, primitive and wicked, simply because they are so remote from our own standard of culture; perhaps, for the same reason, the Yanoáma commit the same mistake when, with the one word 'nape,' they indicate the white man, the foreigner, the wicked man" (1971:14).

On the other side of the world Tuhami, a dark-skinned Arab tilemaker, is being interviewed in the ancient town of Meknes by an anthropologist who has come to Morocco from New York. The year is 1968. Based on his own chronology of the events in Tuhami's life, the American guesses his informant's age to be about 45, although the tilemaker claims ten years more. Age is not the only thing that is indeterminate for the anthropologist, Vincent Crapanzano (1980), who is attempting to record and make sense of Tuhami's life story. The narrative the Moroccan tells is an arabesque of tales in which women— despite the strict segregation of men and women in this traditional Arab society—seek Tuhami out, nurture him, flatter him, and seduce him. But as the tales are retold from time to time, and as Crapanzano presses Tuhami for consistency of detail, the facts give way to revisions in which new episodes are spun out and old ones vanish. In telling about his grandfather, a Muslim from a region below the Sahara, who briefly took responsibility for the boy when his father died and his stepfather refused to take him in, Tuhami recalls the excitement of a trip to Casablanca, where they stayed two months. In a later interview, when Crapanzano asks Tuhami to tell about his first experience with a woman, he responds that is took place in Casablanca when he was there with Mme. Jolan, the European who owns the tile factory where he works and is his patron. He was sixteen. "Mme. Jolan had taken a three months' holiday in Casablanca," Tuhami recounts. "She took me with her. One day she sent me to the market on some errands. I saw a Berber woman at the gate. I winked, and she nodded." Very much surprised, Tuhami asks her why she responded to his wink and she tells him that her husband is a soldier and away. Since Tuhami is a stranger, she says, "I knew there would be no problems." Tuhami goes with her but admits that he doesn't know what to do. The woman instructs him to take off his clothes. She brings him food. He will stay all day and all night, if she has her way. "Who will tell Mme. Jolan?" Tuhami asks. "If I stay, I'll lose my job." The woman says that she will, and they go together at nightfall to the factory owner, who with amusement gives the Berber woman her consent. But the tale is perfectly preposterous! No Moroccan woman would ever agree to such a thing. Several months after telling Crapanzano the story of his love affair with the Berber woman, Tuhami stated that he had been to Casablanca only once—with his grandfather. He no longer even remembered the story of the Berber woman. Now the first woman he had ever slept with was one he met at a saint's tomb at Fez.

On such shifting ground, Crapanzano constructs the biography of Tuhami, increasingly aware as he probes deeper that "the reality of personal history" and "the truth of autobiography" are not necessarily the same. It is not always clear to the anthropologist whether the people in this pious Muslim's account are mortals, demons, or saints. All are quite real to Tuhami, whether they appear in waking life or, as with so many of the important events in his life, when he is asleep and dreaming. Crapanzano never really knows whether or not the women in Tuhami's tales are projections of 'A'isha Qandisha, the camel-footed demoness to whom the tilemaker—like certain other loners or sexual misfits in his culture—is married. Or perhaps, wonders the anthropologist, 'A'isha is the projection of women in real life with whom

Tuhami's relationship has been frustrated. Moroccan men married to 'A'isha can free themselves and master the demoness by plunging a steel knife into the earth when she appears to them. Tuhami has no such knife, and it is an emblem of the anthropologist's willingness to enter the truth of an alternative reality that his parting gift to Tuhami is a steel hunting knife that he will use to gain control of the mistress who continues to haunt him after the anthropologist has gone.

The scope of the life history in anthropology today is well represented by these two narratives. Biocca's (1971) work with Helena Valero emphasizes the importance of recording the direct testimony of those rare individuals who are able to provide us with a vivid picture of life in realms otherwise closed to us as outsiders. Crapanzano's (1980) portrait of Tuhami stresses the art of perceiving truth in experiences branded as lies or delusions in one's own culture. Likewise stressed is the science of recognizing how much of what we know about others (and about ourselves) depends on how the tale is told, to whom, and why. However much the empirical and interpretive aspects of research have been made an arena for recent debates about theory in the social sciences, they are ground that the life-history approach must necessarily span. What person, after all, can count the facts of his or her life without making evaluations about what is important, what good, what painful, what necessary, and what the product of outside forces impersonal or divine? And who could listen to such a story, volunteered or through questioning brought forth, without using the listener's own personal resources for understanding—reason and empathy. The recognition of other more or less successful ways of constituting reality is always threatening, writes Vincent Crapanzano. It may demand a position of extreme cultural relativism and can produce, he says, a sort of "epistemological vertigo." Call it "negotiation," "an encounter," "interaction," or "an exchange"—the collaboration that takes place in the best of life-history work can be for the informant, researcher, and reader a transformative experience.

One purpose of this book is to introduce readers to the full historical and conceptual development of the life-history method in anthropology, especially in the years since L.L. Langness published his earlier discussion (1965b) of this subject. But, as our title reflects, we have decided to talk about the relevance of this method to a wider audience than the life history has usually addressed. An anthropological approach to biography can have a decisive impact not only within the discipline but also, we feel, in such diverse places as literary studies, medical and psychological assessments, case work within the social services, oral histories, policy recommendations or proposed legislation in such fields as mental retardation and gerontology, historical analyses, and the gathering of evidence used to determine the guilt or innocence of alleged offenders brought before the law. Chapter I reviews the growth of professional interest in personal documents as sources of information, at first on life in various cultures and later on the individuals themselves. Readers who want to apply the life-history method in their own work, in or out of anthropology, will find in Chapter II a practical guide to such procedures as selecting an informant, establishing rapport, eliciting narratives and recording them, compiling notes and assembling a final document, and, finally, analyzing the results of these labors. Chapter III looks at specific examples of research in which life histories have been used to answer questions about emotions and cognition, the relationship of personality to culture, child socialization and adult behavior, the life course in this and other societies, mental illness and other forms of deviance, differences in the roles of men and women, and other issues of personal adaptation within the multitude of contexts that shape people's lives. In Chapter IV, we extend this inquiry even further, to consider some of the hidden factors in life histories that until recently have been neglected—such fundamental issues as what a "life" is, what the concepts of a "self" or "person" really mean, and what constraints should be kept in mind when reading and interpreting life-history texts. Finally, in Chapter V, we ask an ethical and moral question that arises from the life-history encounter itself: "Who is doing this biographical work, and why?" The objects of our inquiry are not neutrons, protons, and quarks; they are *people* whom we come to know through the trust they give us. We think it is imperative to indicate the ways in which these people might be put in jeopardy by a researcher's carelessness and, at the same time, to show how the life historian can offer something very precious in return for the trust given.

The approach to describing the lives of ordinary people in their culture that the anthropological life history entails can produce works as powerful and certainly as moving as the Western biographies with which we are already familiar. But the resources that they draw on can make them even more vibrant as pictures of the endlessly varied ways of life that our species has created. It is our hope that professionals and students alike will find in this book a point of view congenial to their own research—an approach that may take them beyond the chronicle of events to a deeper understanding that comes of collaborating to draw essential portraits with skilled eyes and hands.

CHAPTER I

Historical Review

This chapter briefly reviews the use of biography by those in the humanities and in the medical and social sciences. It suggests that the use of biographical techniques is a valuable common denominator for a variety of disciplines. It then reviews the historical importance of biography in the pre-anthropological study of American Indians and during the formative years of American anthropology. Finally, it reviews the anthropological use of life histories to the present time.

*L*ife histories have been an integral part of anthropology at least since the 1920s. But the biographical or life-history method can by no means be considered unique to anthropology. Although the use of biography by anthropologists has a distinctive history, and although certain special problems are involved in the use of biography in the anthropological setting, we believe that much of what we have to say about this method will be useful to a wide variety of investigators in other disciplines, both scientific and humanistic. After all, biography has long been a kind of methodological common denominator in such diverse fields as medicine, sociology, psychology, psychiatry, history, political science, literature, and others, even though little formal attention has been given to this fact. As anthropology is both a humanistic and a scientific enterprise, and as anthropology's range of interest is probably unsurpassed by any other discipline's, it is perhaps the most logical place to attempt a general discussion of the use of biographical methods and techniques.

Biography, as the history of the life of an individual person, is used universally in the humanities and in the psychological, social, and medical sciences, albeit for somewhat different purposes and with varying degrees of success. In history, for example, especially for those historians who subscribe to some variant of the "great man" type of history, biography can be the vehicle through which an entire era is portrayed. William L. Shirer's *The Rise and Fall of the Third Reich* (1960), funamentally a biography of Adolf Hitler, might be seen as a good case in point. Sidney Hook has dealt with biography and history in his well-known book *The Hero in History* (1943), and the American Historical Association published a pamphlet in 1963, "Biography as History" (Mullett 1963), which deals with much the same thing. History was also represented in a monograph commissioned by the Social Science Research Council in 1945 (Gottschalk 1945) that dealt specifically with the potential of biographical methods for the social sciences. Also, recent years have seen the development of an entirely new subfield of history—oral history—in which audio and videotaped biographies and memoirs are recorded for posterity (Bornet 1955; Gluck 1979; Vansina 1965; Wilkie 1967). Similarly, the past half century or so has witnessed the rise of psychohistory, a new interdisciplinary attempt to analyze historical figures. This rather controversial new field has been most importantly linked to Erik Erikson (1975) although the original inspiration must have come from Freud's early analysis of Leonardo da Vinci (1910), which was followed fairly quickly by studies of Amenhotep IV by Abraham (1912), Jones's study of Louis Bonaparte (1913), and others as well. Else Frenkel discussed this development in 1936 in a paper entitled "Studies in Biographic Psychology" (1936). A field related to this is psychobiography, defined recently as "any life history which employs an explicit personality theory" (Glad 1973:296). This would seem to differ from psychohistory mostly in that it does not rely so exclusively on psychoanalytic theory *per se* and in that it deals with contemporary rather than purely historical figures. And whereas psychohistory is most directly associated with the psychoanalytic movement, psychobiography is associated much more with political science.

In literature, of course, biography often forms the core of short stories and novels, and biography itself is considered an art form (Clifford 1962; Kendall 1965). Literary biography is a more specialized field of the same genre (Edel 1959; Nagourney 1978). One need think of only a few of the hundreds of monumental biographical and autobiographical works—*The Education of Henry Adams* (1918), Boswell's *The Life of Samuel Johnson* (1791/1904), *The Confessions of Jean-Jacques Rousseau* (1781), *Everybody's Autobiography* by Gertrude Stein (1937), and H.G. Wells's *Experiment in Autobiography* (1934)—to appreciate the durability and significance of such works. A new interdisciplinary quarterly, *Biography*, created in 1977, attests to the ever increasing interest in the study and appreciation of lives by scholars of all persuasions.

Biographical techniques have been fairly extensively used in sociology at least since the publication of Thomas and Znaniecki's *The Polish Peasant in Europe and America* in 1918. Since about midcentury this interest seems to have turned more toward studies of the life cycle such as "Life Course and Social Structure" (Cain 1964), "Adult Socialization" (Brim 1968) and "Careers" (Becker and Strauss 1956), but quite a number of individual life histories have continued to be produced. There has also been a rapidly increasing interest in aging that has encouraged a life-history approach (Bühler 1935, 1961; Butler 1968; Cumming and Henry 1961; Deutscher 1962; Frank 1980a; Kaufman 1981; Myerhoff 1978, 1979, 1980a, 1980b; Myerhoff and Simić 1978; Vischer 1947; Wrye and Churilla 1977); and older people have been actively encouraged to reminisce and produce biographical accounts as part of the adjustment process (Myerhoff and Tufte 1975). Researchers in the field of mental retardation have been turning to life histories as a means of gathering data on the retarded that would otherwise be lost (Bogdan 1974, 1977; Turner 1980; Whittemore, Koegel, and Langness 1980). Sociological uses of life histories were reviewed by Angell in 1945 (Gottschalk, Kluckhohn, and Angell 1945) and Bogdan (1974, 1977), and Bogdan and Taylor (1975) have dealt with the subject more recently.

In personality psychology, Henry Murray (1938) and his followers and colleagues (Kluckhohn, Murray, and Schneider 1955; White 1952) developed from the 1930s what they termed "the study of lives" and attempted to understand specific research problems, "using a relatively small number of subjects, whose life histories become known through other tests, interviews, and imaginative productions" (White 1964:xiii). Davis and Dollard's *Children of Bondage* (1940) was an important similar work that dealt with the personality development of southern black children. Other interesting leads have been provided more recently by those interested in phenomenology (Bogdan and Taylor 1975; Frank 1979a; Watson 1976, 1978).

In medicine, in general, the first step has long been to elicit biographical information (Blumer 1949). The case-study method has always been integral to psychiatry and clinical psychology. Freud's own classic cases, such as his famous Schreber case, "Psycho-Analytic Notes on an Autobiographical Account of a Case of Paranoia" (1911), and his "Analysis of a Phobia in a Five-Year-Old-Boy" (1909) are perhaps the best examples, but see Adler (1929) and Goldstein and Palmer (1963) for additional ones. Although there are earlier examples such as *Perceval's Narrative* (Bateson 1974), it has only been in the past few years that mental patients and others have been increasingly encouraged or motivated to tell their own stories of hospitalization and treatment, an important perspective not previously much appreciated (Steir 1978). One need only read Carobeth Laird's moving and revealing account of her months in a nursing home, *Limbo* (1979), to understand the importance of such accounts for some much-needed reforms in such institutions.

Anthropologists, especially those interested in psychological anthropology or cultural psychiatry, have employed case studies and life histories to good advantage, especially in the general area of mental illness and its treatment. One of the better examples of this is Gananath

Obeyesekere's extensive account, "Psychocultural Exegesis of a Case of Spirit Possession in Sri Lanka" (1977). For further fairly detailed cases see "Hysterical Psychosis in the New Guinea Highlands: A Bena Bena Example" (Langness 1965a) and the collection, *Case Studies in Spirit Possession* (Crapanzano and Garrison 1977). By far the best full-length treatment in recent years, as readable as it is insightful, is Peter J. Wilson's marvelous *Oscar: An Inquiry Into the Nature of Sanity.* It is Oscar's contention, backed up by Wilson, that "only through the study of the extraordinary can we come to some sort of understanding of the ordinary" (1975:4). Oscar, who is quite extraordinary, has much to tell us about the interface of culture, society, and the individual.

Neurotic and psychotic episodes, hallucinations, dreams, fantasies, and "wishes of the soul" are all phenomena that demand a biographical approach, but until recent years these were not an important area for anthropological research. And even since the advent of "psychological anthropology," life histories have only rarely been employed to research them. Although interest in life history research has picked up of late, its potential has still not been fully exploited. And while Kluckhohn's gloomy assessment of 1945, repeated by Langness after his survey of 1965 (1965b) is not entirely applicable at the present, there remains much that could be done. We believe that part of the resistance to the more extensive use of life histories has to do with problems of method and analysis inherent in the approach itself, as well as factors associated with anthropological fieldwork in general.

The Early Period in Anthropology

Although there was considerable interest in American Indians from the initial period of European contact onward there was no profession of anthropology as we know it until approximately 1900, and even then anthropology as an academic discipline and profession grew rather slowly. According to Kluckhohn, who reviewed the use of biography in anthropology in 1945, the first personal accounts of American Indians published specifically as such by an anthropologist were three war narratives brought out by A.L. Kroeber in 1908 (Kluckhohn 1945:86). There was a considerable body of biographical materials on American Indians before this time, however, published by a variety of writers with their own interests and motives.

During the nineteenth century in America, the frontiers were rapidly vanishing and the last of the great Indian wars finally ground to their bitterly unpleasant end at the massacre on December 29, 1890, known as the Battle of Wounded Knee (Brown 1971). There was great popular interest in the lives and personalities of American Indians, particularly those who received publicity or notoriety of any kind. This interest expressed itself in attendance at "Wild West Shows" and the reading of "dime novels" that generally portrayed the Indian as a savage bent upon nothing other than murder, rape, and pillage. Apologists for the treatment afforded Indians at the hands of the European latecomers likewise portrayed the Indian in the most unpleasant light. But there was always a certain ambivalence on the part of many, and Indians were not totally without defenders who portrayed them as "noble savages," unfairly treated and preyed upon by greedy and rapacious whites. This ambivalence can be seen in this comment by Mark Twain:

> He is noble. He is true and loyal; not even imminent death can shake his peerless faithfulness. His heart is a well-spring of truth, and of generous impulses, and of knightly magnanimity. With him gratitude is religion; do him a kindness, and at the end of a lifetime he has not forgotten it.

> He is ignoble—base and treacherous, and hateful in every way. Not even imminent death can startle him into a spasm of virtue. . . . His heart is a cesspool of falsehood, of treachery, and of low and devilish instincts. With him, gratitude is an unknown emotion; and when one does him a kindness, it is safest to keep the face toward him, lest the reward be an arrow in the back.

> —Mark Twain, "The Noble Red Man"

Among American writers only Hawthorne and Melville seem to have recognized and dealt openly with the racism involved in the portrayal of American Indians (Barnett 1975). And those who wished to attract white settlers into virgin territory were not beyond glorifying the Indian for their own advantage (Savage 1977). In general, however, as Philip Borden remarked, "The nineteenth century had opened with Americans holding a notion of the Indian as a beast. It was closing with the idea of the Indian as a retarded child" (Borden 1970:96).

When it came to biographical materials, naturally enough Indian chiefs or famous warriors were the most popular subject matter, with Christianized Indians probably being next in interest. This can be seen in the following brief chronology of works which also indicate the unbroken interest in the lives of American Indians from the earliest historical time right up to the present. Perhaps the earliest known biographical work on a North American Indian was a *Memoir of Catherine Brown, a Christian Indian of the Cherokee Nation* published prior to 1825 (Anderson 1825). In 1832 B.B. Thatcher published *Indian Biography: Or, An Historical Account of Those Individuals Who Have Been Distinguished Among the North American Natives as Orators, Warriors, Statesmen and Other Remarkable Characters*. In 1841 Andrew Welch published an account of Oceola Nikkanouchee—the famous Seminole resistance leader Osceola. In 1843 there appeared an anonymous volume called *Lives of Celebrated American Indians*. An account of an Ojibwa chief was published in 1867 (Enimikeeso). Also during this early period, and later as well, artists and travelers supplemented their sketches and paintings with brief biographical remarks about their subjects. J.M. Stanley (1852) is perhaps the best example of this.

Somewhat later Dodd, Mead and Company began publishing a series called *Famous American Indians* (Eggleston and Seelye 1878, 1879), and in 1891 there appeared a kind of "Who's Who" of leading men of the Indian territory modestly entitled *Leaders and Leading Men of the Indian Territory With Interesting Biographical Sketches* (O'Beirne). A life of Sitting Bull appeared in the same year (Johnson) but by this time there were already many full-length biographical accounts of famous Indians including Tecumseh of the Shawanoe (Drake 1841), Red Jacket of the Seneca (Hubbard 1886; Stone 1841), Black Hawk of the Sac (Drake 1854, Patterson 1882), Pontiac of the Ottawa (Ellis 1861), Brant of the Mohawk (Anonymous 1872; Stone 1865), Chief Joseph of the Nez Perce (Howard 1881; Lowe 1881), and Se-Quo-Yah, who had innovated the Cherokee syllabary writing (Foster 1885). There were doubtless others which have escaped our attention. Samuel Drake's *The Aboriginal Races of North America* (1880), which included biographical sketches, ran to at least 15 editions. The three volume work of McKenny and Hall, *The Indian Tribes of North America, With Biographical Sketches and Anecdotes of the Principal Chiefs*, first came out in 1836 and was reprinted as late as 1933.

There were early autobiographical accounts as well as biographical ones. Indeed, there were at least five of them prior to 1850 (Anderson 1825; Apes 1831; Black Hawk 1834; Cuffe 1839; and Copway 1847). All of these with one exception were by highly acculturated individuals who had been influenced by missionaries. The exception is by a Sauk war leader and constitutes a plea for an end to white aggression toward the Indians and an attempt to justify his own conduct in warfare. All of the volumes bear much evidence of white supervision and editing.

Although biographical materials by anthropologists do not appear until the 1900s, the popular interest in the lives of Indians has continued unabated to the present. In 1900 there was a life of Samson Occum (Love). *Life of Apushimata* (Lincecum) was published in 1906 along with *Geronimo's Story of His Life* (Barrett) and *Lives of Famous Indian Chiefs* (Wood). In 1916, *The Princess Pocahontas* (Watson) appeared and was followed in the next year by *Ka-Mi-Akin, Last Hero of the Yakimas* (Splawn). In 1931 (Chapin) and 1938 (Britt) there appeared still further volumes dealing with a number of Indian chiefs. Unusually well-documented biographies came out at about this time on Sequoyah (Foreman 1938), Sacajawea (Hebard 1933), and Pocahontas (Garnett 1933). Frank Linderman wrote two popular and somewhat sentimental accounts (1930, 1932) and Stanley Vestal wrote two interesting accounts of Sitting Bull (1932) and White Bull (1934).

At about this time appeared four volumes of personal reminiscences by three different Sioux Indians themselves (Eastman 1902; Neihardt 1932; Standing Bear 1928, 1933). Additional biographies of Chief Joseph appeared in 1936 (Fee) and 1941 (Howard), and a new biography of Tecumseh in 1938 (Oskison). Yellow Wolf, a Nez Perce, told his story for publication during this period (McWhorter 1940). Heluiz Washburne published an exceptional "autobiography" of an Eskimo woman in the same year (1940). In 1941 Zimmerman published on White Eagle, a Ponca chief, and in 1943 biographies of Chief Seattle (Anderson) and Black Hawk (Beals) appeared. In 1951 an account of famous Indians who visited Washington, D.C., and called on the White House was published (Turner). In 1953 still another, *Chief Joseph of the Nez Perce* (Garst) was published. New books on Joseph Brant (Chalmers) and Tecumseh (Tucker) appeared in 1955 and 1956 respectively. In 1962 a new book on Yellow Wolf was published (Chalmers) and in 1963 a new and excellent popular historical biography of Chief Joseph and the Nez Perce war appeared (Beal). In 1955 the text of the first edition of Black Hawk's autobiography was republished after a period of more than 100 years (Jackson). *I, Nuligak*, the personal account of a Canadian Eskimo, came out in English in 1966 (Nuligak); *Karnee: A Paiute*

Narrative, the Story of Annie Lowry (Scott) did also. *Jim Whitewolf: The Life of a Kiowa Apache Indian* appeared in 1969 (Brant) and John Neihardt brought out a new version of the life of the Sioux Eagle Voice in 1970. *Lame Deer: Seeker of Visions* came out in 1972 (Lame Deer and Erdoes) and N. Scott Momaday published his "imaginative autobiogaphy" in 1976.

This is hardly an exhaustive list and it says nothing of the many informative reminiscences of white pioneers or the thousands of articles and newspaper accounts that have dealt with American Indian personalities. The unprecedented success of Theodora Kroeber's fine work, *Ishi in Two Worlds* (1961), for a book of its kind, suggests perhaps more than any other criterion the high degree of popular interest that remains in the American Indian (and the "exotic") when presented in an accessible and biographical format.

We have concentrated here on American Indians primarily because the life-history method in anthropology emerged out of research on American Indians. But of course there has been both a professional and a popular interest in the lives of people of other cultures as well. Similarly, readers seem to have always been interested in the lives of "deviants" or unusual people of most any kind. Some further cross-cultural works of quite exceptional merit, although not written by anthropologists, include: Ntara's *Man of Africa* (1934), Gollock's *Lives of Eminent Africans* (1928), *Ten Africans* (Perham 1936), Sachs's famous *Black Hamlet* (1937), and *Turi's Book of Lappland* (Hatt 1931). Such interests appear to have intensified in recent years, stimulated, it would seem, by the civil rights and various liberation movements. Claude Brown's *Manchild in the Promised Land* (1965) and Malcolm X's *The Autobiography of Malcolm X* (1966) are probably the best known of such nonprofessional works by American blacks, but the many others include Dick Gregory's powerful *Nigger: An Autobiography* (1964). Recent interesting works on women include Cornelisen's moving *Women of the Shadows* (1976) and Grönoset's unusual account of a Norwegian peasant woman, *Anna* (1975). There is also the unusual work by Maxine Hong Kingston, *The Woman Warrior* (1976), an autobiographical and also allegorical account dealing with women's rights and her own socialization as an American Chinese. Accounts of the lives of the poor include *Hard Living on Clay Street: Portraits of Blue Collar Families* (Howell 1973), *Poor Americans: How the White Poor Live* (Pilisuk 1971), and *The Whole Works: The Autobiography of a Young American Couple* (Krueger 1973). Accounts of American Japanese include *The Two Worlds of Jim Yoshida* (Yoshida 1962), *Nisei Daughter* (Sone 1953), *American in Disguise* (Okimoto 1971), John Okada's (1976) autobiographical novel of internment in an American concentration camp in World War II, and Kikumura's moving and thoughtful reflections on the life of her Issei mother, *Through Harsh Winters: The Story of a Japanese Immigrant Woman* (1981). Jade Snow Wong's *Fifth Chinese Daughter* (1950) remains as one of the better nonprofessional autobiographies of an American Chinese woman. There continue to be hundreds of biographies of and autobiographies by all kinds of people and about all kinds of people published each year. We seem never to lose our curiosity about each other and our desire to know the myriad details, occasional disasters, and constant turnings that combine together in different contexts to make up what we perceive as our "lives." Clyde Kluckhohn pointed out in 1945 (1945:83) that whatever potential these many nonprofessional documents might have for anthropologists has never been exploited. He attributed this omission to the notorious failure of anthropologists to do library research. These various works perhaps do contain useful information that social scientists could exploit in their search to understand the relationship of individuals to their society and culture, but they continue to be either ignored by anthropologists or, at best, neglected.

1920 to 1945

Gordon Allport marks the publication of *The Polish Peasant* in 1920 as the turning point in the critical use of life history documents in psychology and sociology (1942:18). The beginning of truly rigorous work in the field of biography by professional anthropologists is probably most conveniently marked by the publication in 1926 of Paul Radin's well-known work, *Crashing Thunder*. There had been, of course, some work of a professional nature earlier, but this did not take the form of serious full-length life studies. Radin had published, as early as 1913, a brief autobiography of a Winnebago Indian. In 1920 he published a considerably longer one, which ultimately became *Crashing Thunder*, in which he argued that biographical information was needed to supplement the more usual anthropological accounts:

> . . . the aim being, not to obtain autobiographical details about some definite personage, but to have some representative middle-aged individual of

moderate ability describe his life in relation to the social group in which he had grown up. (1920:384)

The Handbook of American Indians North of Mexico (Hodge 1907) contains several brief biographical sketches. As has been mentioned, three brief war narratives were brought out by Kroeber in 1908. In 1919 Wallis used personal narratives in his account of the Sun Dance and Edward Sapir published a short life of a Nootka Indian in 1921.

Sapir's work, unlike that of Radin and the others, seems to reflect a growing interest in the individual, as such, at this time, rather than the more traditional interest in culture. This interest seems to have been stimulated at least in part by developments of German ethnography in the early 1900s. Schmidt, in 1906, an important representative of German anthropology, made a specific plea for more studies of the individual. Koppers in 1924, following in this tradition, published personal sketches of Tierra del Fuegians in a popular account of his fieldwork. He also included a paper on the investigation of individuals in the *Festschrift* volume he edited in honor of Schmidt in 1928. Franz Boas, who had been educated in Germany and was Sapir's mentor, had a long-standing interest in the individual which he doubtless communicated to Sapir, but Sapir's growing interest in psychiatry, and in the relationship of psychiatry to anthropology, was perhaps a more important factor in leading him to emphasize the importance of the individual.

A somewhat different goal was pursued by Gilbert Wilson, who presented at about this same period some documents which, according to Kluckhohn, "are among the most distinguished and the most neglected products of American ethnology" (1945:88). At an early date Wilson attempted to present what today would be termed the ethos of Hidatsa culture, that is, the underlying philosophical and emotional tone of the culture as seen through the eyes of his informants themselves (1917, 1924, 1928). He also produced an "autobiography," *Goodbird the Indian: His Story* (n.d.), but it was for more popular consumption and contained considerable missionary propaganda. Truman Michelson was another who contributed importantly to the growing body of Indian biography. Michelson wrote "autobiographies" of three native women, one a Fox (1925), one a Cheyenne (1932) and one an Arapaho (1933). These were unusual in a discipline that was traditionally heavily male-oriented and is only just now beginning to redress the balance.

Another trend was apparent at this time, similar but not identical to that discussed above: an attempt to "humanize" anthropological materials and present them to a wider audience. This influence can be seen earliest in Adolph Bandelier's novel of the Pueblos, *The Delight Makers* (1890), but more importantly in *American Indian Life*, a volume edited by Elsie Clews Parsons in 1922. *American Indian Life* included the biographical sketch published the year previously by Sapir, several shorter biographical sketches, and a variety of other materials. Parsons had herself published brief biographical sketches in previous years (1919, 1921). More or less the same kind of general approach can be seen in Rasmussen (1908), Austin's three-act play (1915), Barbeau (1928), Grinnell (1920), Harrington (1933), and Radin (1927a). This trend might be said to have reached a peak of sorts with the publication of Oliver La Farge's Pulitzer Prize winning *Laughing Boy* (1929), a fictionalized account of the lives of the Navaho couple Laughing Boy and Slim Girl as they were affected by culture contact.

Prior to the 1930s American anthropology was, relatively speaking, nontheoretical and suspicious of the grandiose evolutionary theories of culture that had emerged from the previous century. Franz Boas had virtually singlehandedly trained a generation of anthropologists who were, with some exceptions, more concerned with collecting and recording ethnographic facts than with analyzing them. The theoretical impact of Radcliffe-Brown and Malinowski had not yet made itself completely felt, and Sapir's influence was only beginning to come into its own. There was the consciously expressed belief that since American Indian cultures were fast disappearing it was critical to salvage as much as possible. Analyses could come later, after all the data were safely tucked away in archives and museums. Many scholars were engaged on the reservations and elsewhere in this type of recording and in many cases there were few available informants who were able to tell the ethnographer in any articulate, integrated manner just what the traditional way of life had been like. Given this situation, it is not surprising that Radin looked for a "representative middle-aged individual" and, later, a "primitive philosopher" (1927b). Furthermore, until about this same time, there was little explicit concern with the methodology of ethnographic fieldwork. This began to change and a genuine improvement in published life histories came about as a result.

Some of the improvement was doubtless the result of John Dollard's

Criteria for the Life History (1935), which for the first time focused directly on the methodological problems involved in the use of life histories. It is interesting to note that Dollard's work, like Radin's rather than Sapir's, reflects the general interest of the period in using life histories to illuminate cultural and social facts instead of individual lives or aspects of personality. Indeed, Dollard devoted himself almost exclusively to showing the importance of the culture concept and how biography must be seen in a cultural rather than purely psychological dimension. Gordon Allport later criticized Dollard for his "cultural bias" (1942), but this in no way detracts from the great interest stimulated by Dollard's insightful and timely work.

In addition to book reviews of biographical and autobiographical documents, which naturally were concerned with methodological considerations, there appeared during this period many articles in anthropology, sociology, and psychology dealing with the more specific problems of fieldwork and the taking of life histories. Social scientists were becoming increasingly self-conscious about their methods. Paul Radin brought out a volume on methodology in 1933. Margaret Mead suggested more comprehensive field methods in 1933 and in 1939 wrote on the problems involved in the use of native languages as fieldwork tools. This prompted quick replies from Elkin (1941), Lowie (1940), and Henry (1940). Lowie in his fine work on the Crow (1935) had commented earlier on the problems of using American Indian languages. In 1937, Reckless and Selling compared psychiatric and sociological interviewing, and Cora DuBois wrote on psychological objectives and techniques in ethnography. Schapera wrote on field methods for studying culture contact (1935). S.F. Nadel wrote a brief article on problems of interviewing (1939) and Richards did an essay in the same year on the development of fieldwork methods. Blumer prepared an extensive critique of *The Polish Peasant* at the request of the Social Science Research Council in 1939 and in the same year Cartwright and French questioned the reliability of life-history materials. Then in 1940 an article on the participant-observer technique by Florence Kluckhohn appeared, and in 1942 Herbert Passin wrote a perceptive article on prevarication as a problem in fieldwork. In 1945 the Social Science Research Council sponsored new work on the use of personal documents, which remained a definitive account for many years (C. Kluckhohn). It is worth the effort even now to consider Clyde

Kluckhohn's summary of life-history data and generalizations up
to 1945:

1. A considerable number of popular and historical biographical and
   autobiographical documents, of widely varying quality, exist. These
   have not as yet been systematically exploited by anthropologists.
2. The number of professional studies is steadily growing. However, the
   following limitations upon the adequacy of existent materials must be
   recognized:
   (a) The vast majority are too sketchy and too limited to objective
       events. They do not give even the shadow of a life—merely the
       partially outlined skeleton,
   (b) The different age and sex groups are very unevenly represented.
       Almost all of the subjects were fifty years of age or over at the time of
       giving their autobiography, and the vast majority are men.
   (c) With the exception of about half a dozen tribes, there is no basis for
       comparison of life histories within the same culture and hence of
       judging whether or not a particular document is a representative
       sample.
   (d) Annotation is very meager and almost exclusively of an ethno-
       graphic character. Analysis and interpretation have only begun to
       appear.
   (e) The conditions under which and the techniques by which data have
       been obtained are very inadequately specified.
   (f) Published biographical materials are, at best, only very generally
       and roughly comparable because conditions and techniques are
       either unknown or, where at least partially described, so very
       different.

Nonetheless, stimulated by and associated with the methodological
questions being raised, there were some fine professional documents
produced during this period: Dyk's *Son of Old Man Hat* (1938),
Underhill's "autobiography" of a Papago woman (1936), Gorer's work
on the Lepchas (1938), *Smoke from Their Fires* by Ford (1941), and *Sun Chief*
by Simmons (1942), to mention the better-known ones. Both Ruth
Landes (1938) and Morris Opler (1938a, 1938b, 1941) made use of
biographical materials at this time, as also did Redfield and Villa (1934),
Julian Steward (1938), and Leslie White (1943). F.E. Williams recorded
the reminiscences of Ahuia Ova (1939), and Gladys Reichard wrote a
slightly fictionalized biographical account of a Navaho woman (1939)
which had been preceded by a similar attempt in 1934.

Form this period on, anthropology in general became much more concerned with both method and theory than it had been. Developments in the 1930s led to the rise of two competing but both highly theoretical trends—British social anthropology, and a more psychologically inclined American anthropology (Spiro 1972). It might be expected that in the American tradition at least, with its emphasis on personality, there would have been an increased interest in the use of life histories; and indeed, there was, but only on the part of a very few. The most sophisticated and conscious attempt to use life histories for the study of culture and personality can be seen in the related works of Cora DuBois, *The People of Alor* (1944), and Abram Kardiner, *The Psychological Frontiers of Society* (1945). The thesis of primary institutions (such as childrearing practices) and secondary institutions (such as religious practices) as cultural variables being linked by personality attributes (psychological variables) was an important theoretical landmark, the acceptance of which made the use of life histories virtually a necessity. Consider this brief excerpt from *The Psychological Frontiers of Society*:

> For the purpose of substantiating the thesis of this book one biography in a culture will hardly suffice. We must have an adequate sampling of sex, age, and status differentiations, and no arbitrary number can be regarded as adequate. We need a sufficient number to make adequate comparisons, but it is more important to find where the deviations are. As we progress in our study of biographies we note the banal fact that no two in the same culture are alike. But the deviants are as important to us as the norms.
>
> The uses of the biographies are numerous. Here is our first chance to see whether our guess about the kind of personality a given set of institutions will create is at all approximated in reality. We can reverse the procedure and operate from personalities to institutions. It is only in a biography that we can see how the various institutions are functionally articulated. (Kardiner 1945:37)

Notice here that the interest in culture is not given up in favor of an interest in personality. Rather, an interest in personality is added to the earlier anthropological interest. The work of Kardiner, Linton, DuBois, and the other collaborators was not without its effect on subsequent anthropology, and a position similar to theirs but somewhat more sophisticated is still much in evidence. Their emphasis on life histories, however, has not been followed and, although many life histories have been produced since this time, they spring mostly from different motives.

1945 to the Present

The biographical studies produced by anthropologists, when they are not attempting to answer some theoretical question in psychological anthropology, tend to be used for one or more of the following reasons: (1) to portray culture, (2) for literary purposes, (3) to portray aspects of culture change, (4) to illustrate some aspect of culture not usually portrayed by other means (such as women's view of their culture); (5) to communicate something not otherwise communicated (for example, the humanistic side of anthropology or, more typically, the "insider's" view of culture); or (6) to say something about deviants or other unusual cases.

In studies designed to portray a culture, following Radin's lead, a person is usually selected who is taken to be the most representative member. One of the better examples of this type of work is *Juan the Chamula* by Ricardo Pozas (1962). According to the author, this book "should be considered a small monograph on the culture of the Chamulas" (1962:1). In addition the book attempts to give some insight into the process of culture change. A similar use of biographical materials, on a smaller scale, can be seen in an article by Robert Glasse (1959). He attempts to give an idea of certain details of Huli culture (a Papua New Guinea group) by using three male life histories selected as highly representative of three different status positions. When Dyk published his well-known *Son of Old Man Hat* he specifically wanted to get at "Navaho life in general" by using a "long slow narrative that recalled the ordinary, the petty, the humdrum insignificant affairs" (as well as anecdotes about highly dramatic events) (1938:xi). Many, if not most, of the earlier anthropological life histories had the portrayal of culture as their primary if not only goal.

From a literary as well as an anthropological standpoint Oscar Lewis has been beyond question the greatest proponent of the life history, although that was not his only purpose in developing his life histories. *Five Families* (1959) represented a valuable innovation in ethnological research and led to *The Children of Sánchez* (1961) and to his subsequent books, which raised the life-history approach to a distinctive and recognized literary genre. *The Children of Sánchez* is not only a literary masterpiece but also a valuable cultural document, and by using multiple life histories as he did, Lewis at least partially overcame some of the previous objections to the life history approach:

In my research in Mexico since 1943, I have attempted to develop a number of approaches to family studies. In *Five Families*, I tried to give the reader some glimpses of daily life in five ordinary Mexican families, on five perfectly ordinary days. In this volume I offer the reader a deeper look into the lives of one of these families by the use of a new technique whereby each member of the family tells his own life story in his own words. This approach gives us a cumulative, multifaceted, panoramic view of each individual, of the family as a whole, and of many aspects of lower-class Mexican life. The independent versions of the same incidents given by the various family members provide a built-in check upon the reliability and validity of much of the data and thereby partially offset the subjectivity inherent in a single autobiography.

At the same time it reveals the discrepancies in the way the events are recalled by each member of the family.

This method of multiple autobiographies also tends to reduce the element of investigator bias because the accounts are not put through the sieve of a middle-class North American mind but are given in the words of the subjects themselves. In this way, I believe I have avoided the two most comon hazards in the study of the poor, namely, oversentimentalization and brutalization. Finally, I hope that this method preserves for the reader the emotional satisfaction and understanding which the anthropologist experiences in working directly with his subjects but which is only rarely conveyed in the formal jargon of anthropological monographs. (1961:xi)

Expressed here is Lewis's interest in the culture of poverty (a concept he invented which, although controversial, generated much further work and interest), and in communicating to the reader some of the more humanistic dimensions of anthropological research. *The Children of Sánchez* and Lewis's later *Pedro Martinez* (1964) remain among the very best of the biographical studies produced by anthropologists. There recently appeared a three-volume oral history of contemporary Cuba which is a result of and an extension of Lewis's biographical and other researches and his interest in the culture of poverty (Lewis, Lewis, and Rigdon 1977a, 1977b, 1978). The first volume, *Four Men* (1977a), concentrates on the effects of the revolution on four men raised in poverty and living in shanty towns. Their exceedingly rich accounts of their lives give the reader not only a genuine feeling for how the revolution affected them but also a comprehensive picture of their daily lives and their culture. *Four Women* (1977b) is a similar work although the four women involved are not all from poverty backgrounds. These two works, read along with the third volume, *Neighbors* (1978), give a truly comprehensive appreciation of what the revolution has meant to ordinary Cubans, how it has affected sex roles and occupations, how fast culture change can actually occur under such circumstances, and how it is that individual lives affect and are in turn affected by institutional and social processes. *Neighbors* employs the same technique of interviewing numerous family members that Lewis pioneered in *Five Families* and deals, again, with five families, in this case families sharing an apartment house in Havana. This technique does in fact preserve for the reader "the emotional satisfaction and understanding the anthropologist experiences in working directly" with subjects and is, in addition, an incredibly rich source of basic ethnographic information. An important book of related interest is Margaret Randall's *Cuban Women Now: Interviews with Cuban Women* (1974).

One of the finest biographies to focus specifically on issues of cultural change is Sidney Mintz's *Worker in the Cane* (1960). Although without quite the literary power of Lewis's work, Mintz's "autobiography" of a poor Puerto Rican middle-aged man gives an extraordinarily rich account of cultural and political change. Mintz makes no pretensions about how representative his case is although he does say it is "the autobiography of an average man" (1960:ix).

Another study of an "ordinary Navaho" which also deals with culture change is Crapanzano's *The Fifth World of Enoch Maloney: Portrait of a Navaho* (1969). This is not, strictly speaking, a biography but, rather, as the title suggests, a portrait. In this case, the portrait is drawn from Crapanzano's field notes and consists of his own and others' dealings with Enoch over a period of approximately two months. A second aim of the book is to communicate something of the experience of field work. A very slightly altered version of this book appeared again in 1972 as *The Fifth World of Forster Bennett*.

One of the better attempts to use a life history for the purpose of illuminating culture change is John G. Kennedy's *Struggle for Change in a Nubian Community*. Quoting C. Wright Mills, Kennedy states his purpose as follows: "Neither the life of an individual nor the history of a society can be understood without understanding both. . . . By the fact of his living, [an individual] contributes, however minutely, to the shaping of his society, and to the course of its history, even as his is made by society and by its historical push and shove" (1977:12). Far from being an average individual, the subject of Kennedy's life history is a most unusual man who had a disproportionate and significant effect upon the directions of his changing culture.

It is probably safe to say that all anthropological life histories deal in some way with culture change, as the very presence of the fieldworker is an indication of change and it is unlikely that both interviewer and interviewee would fail to discuss it.

Life histories of women have increased in number in the past few years and this increase is mostly due to the attempt to portray what was more traditionally a "neglected aspect of culture." An interesting "non-professional" attempt to present a woman's view was *Zulu Woman* by Rebecca Reyher (1948), who posed somewhat empathically the following questions:

> What did Zulu women do? How did they manage lifelong marriage? Were they happy? Was polygamy, as my sophisticated friends assured me, a natural state of man? Was it possible to love with one's body freely and easily, capturing the spirit and taming it to its primary needs? Didn't Zulu women get notions too? Were the heart and soul of a primitive woman different from mine, or those of women I knew? (1948:xii)

Also published in 1948 was Alice Marriott's *Maria: The Potter of San Ildefonso*, an interesting account of selected aspects of a woman's life.

One of the better full-length autobiographies of women, *Baba of Karo,* appeared in 1954. In addition to giving a woman's perspective, it

> . . . is valuable from two different points of view: as a record of Hausa life it is unique in detail, the time span, the variety of aspects and events, and above all in its immediacy; but is is significant also to the social anthropologist with structural interests as a documentation of the extent to which, and the precise way in which, structure governs and shapes an individual life. A great deal has recently been written on a variety of postulated relationships between "culture" and "personality"; this record will have served a useful function if it suggests ways in which the individual's life process and its relations to the social structure can be studied in greater detail with a diachronic perspective. (Smith 1954:14)

In 1961, Nancy Lurie published *Mountain Wolf Woman*, an especially valuable account in that the subject was the sister of Radin's subject, Crashing Thunder. John Blacking produced an especially sensitive account of a South African girl, *Black Background: The Childhood of a South African Girl* in 1964. Blacking combined his own ethnographic knowledge of Venda culture with the short sketches of a 17-year-old Venda girl and the result is a very pleasing if "tiny slice of their fascinating culture."

A recent work, *Nine Mayan Women* (Elmendorf 1976), although it deals most importantly with culture change, also, according to the foreword by Alfonso Villa Rojas, "permits us to approach very closely the world of the Mayan woman, with its constellations of usages, customs, practices, and attitudes towards love, desires and frustrations, reticences and confidences" (1976:xv). *Yaqui Women: Contemporary Life Histories* by Jane Holden Kelley (1978) is an exceptionally fine account of four Yaqui women as they survived the Yaqui wars and deportation. Few, if any, accounts by "outsiders," however, can approach the significance and power of a book like *Child of the Dark*, Carolina Maria De Jesus's terrifying diary account of her life in the slums of São Paulo (1962).

One of the most successful attempts to present an inside view of another culture is the remarkable autobiography, *Two Leggings*, by Peter Nabokov (1967). Using an early manuscript prepared by William Wildschut for the Museum of the American Indian, Heye Foundation, plus the ethnographic materials available for the Crow Indian, Nabokov produced an "autobiographical" account that gives much insight into the values and motivations that drove the Crow to exceptional acts of bravery and endurance in their warlike society. It also demonstrates the relationship between Crow religious beliefs and the pursuit of personal power and success. It is much to our benefit that Wildschut recognized Two Leggings's account as a "primary source for an understanding of Crow Indian life" and recorded it when he did.

Another work that states as its primary goal the presentation of an "insider's" point of view is *Beyond the Mountains of the Moon* by Edward H. Winter:

> The four people—two men, Kihara and Mpuga, and two women, Lubangi and Kike, the wives of Mpuga—with whose lives we are concerned, are members of a group known as the Amba who live behind a great range of mountains on the western borders of Uganda.
>
> When one first enters their universe it is as though one had walked through the looking glass. Their lives differ from those of the people with whom most of us are familiar in at least two important respects. The situation in which they find themselves is different; different things happen to them and different things are expected of them. Over and above this they perceive situations and events in a way which is foreign to us. This different way of looking at things is most difficult for the student of primitive people to communicate to others. I believe, however, that in life histories of this sort the people themselves are able to convey some understanding of it. (1965:1)

To present the insider's view of a culture has long been one of the stated goals of the profession of anthropology and of those who have provided life histories. Anthropologists have achieved this with varying degrees of success. Certainly the use of life histories would seem especially compatible for this purpose although, as we shall see later, it is not quite as simple as it appears. For an unusually insightful and successful attempt to portray the insider's view of the difficulties of upper-class women in a changing society see *Bengali Women* by Manisha Roy (1975), herself a Bengali woman and also a well-trained and sensitive anthropologist. Lewis, Lewis, and Rigdon's *Four Women* (1977b) is similarly valuable in giving this insider's perspective.

One sees in this brief historical review the attempts by anthropologists and others to come to grips with a variety of issues through the explicit use of biographical and life-history materials. Although, as is clear enough, this has been a long-standing interest on the part of many, these attempts taken collectively have not been as systematic as they might have been, there has been little or no interdisciplinary collaboration, and in general much more attention has been devoted to description than to analysis. Even in what might be seen as the very best of these life-history accounts the role of the investigator, whether as field worker, writer-editor, or analyst, has seldom been considered. Although this is a glaring omission for any type of biographer, it is particularly problematic for anthropologists because of the nature of the fieldwork process itself.

CHAPTER II

Methods

As life histories by anthropologists usually emerge out of the fieldwork situation, in this chapter we discuss the methods and techniques involved in the process of anthropological fieldwork in general and life history taking in particular. Problems of rapport, language, interviewing, reliability, sampling, note-taking and other such matters are examined. The collaborative nature of the work is emphasized.

*A*lthough anthropologists occasionally produce life histories on the basis of interview materials alone, more often the life histories emerge from the fieldwork context itself. Accordingly, and as anthropologists believe that a knowledge of context is crucial for understanding, we deem it important to discuss anthropological fieldwork in general as well as life-history taking in particular. Indeed, the two processes have a great deal in common, and one of the recurring flaws in existing life histories is the failure to discuss the fieldwork situation out of which they emerged. Just what was the relationship of investigator to subject? How long was the investigator in the field? How much does he or she know about the subject from personal observation? How much from other people who know the subject? Under what circumstances did they come by their information? What was *their* relationship to the subject? Under what circumstances did they confide it to you, the anthropologist? What are the physical, social, and cultural features that surround the person's life? How did you, the investigator, go about finding out such things? Anthropological fieldwork, of which life-history taking is a part, is an exceedingly complex and difficult process. It is, above all, a *collaborative* enterprise, a fact of great importance that until fairly recently has been rather neglected.

Anthropological data are acquired almost exclusively through fieldwork. Anthropological fieldwork is conducted by the repeated performance of five fundamental tasks: watching, asking, listening, sometimes *doing*, and recording. The process of life-history taking is essentially the same. It would appear to be simple enough but it is, in practice, exceedingly difficult and fraught with many possibilities for error. The data accumulated in this way can range from the most simple observation of the most mundane artifact to a complex description of the most complete and exotic religious system, none of which has actually been observed by the fieldworker. It is probably safe to infer that the more the data are based upon direct observation the more accurate they are, while the more they are based upon what one has been told the less accurate they are. Indeed, one of the traditional objections to life histories has been that they usually rely exclusively on verbal accounts by a single individual that are difficult or impossible to verify. The problems involved stem mostly from the personal biases and beliefs of both observer and observed. This fact has led in the past to the rejection of introspective accounts and to the development of extreme forms of behaviorism—and to a suspicion of the life-history method. As a science, anthropology demands, however, that all human behavior, introspective as well as any other, be taken into account. Although anthropologists can do and on rare occasions actually have done controlled observations without verbal accounts and introspection, this procedure ignores what are by far the most interesting and important aspects of human behavior. Whether one is dedicated to anthropology as "an experimental science in search of laws," as most have been and many still are, or believes it is "an interpretive one in search of meaning" as do Geertz and others (1973:5), it is impossible to deny that anthropologists must be concerned with "action" as well as "behavior." Here we follow Reynolds, who makes this distinction:

> If we describe what people or animals do, without inquiring into their subjective reasons for doing it, we are talking about their *behaviour*. If we study the subjective aspects of what they do, the reasons and ideas underlying and guiding it, then we are concerned with the world of *meaning*. if we concern ourselves both with what people are, overtly and objectively, seen to do (or not to do) and their reasons for so doing (or not doing) which relate to the world of meaning and understanding, we then describe action. (1976:xv)

We might well say we are also describing lives. Ideally, anthropological fieldworkers would like to have actually witnessed, participated in, and had explained to them every significant event that occurs in someone's life as well as how those events occurred in the particular culture selected for study. For practical reasons such an ideal is never attained. For example, it is entirely possible and sometimes happens that during, say, a year in the field, no one dies and hence no funeral can be witnessed. Similarly, it is even more possible that in societies with elaborate initiation ceremonies, no initiation will be held during the anthropologist's tenure, or no one will get married, and so on. What the fieldworker takes home, then, is a record of all the events seen, plus descriptions and explanations of them by informants, plus a great many more descriptions of things not seen. Always, the fieldworker has information about many more things than have actually been witnessed. This statement applies particularly to life histories. Because researchers can know these things only through the words of their informants or through their own eyes, because informants understand them only as they relate to their own unique history, and also because ethnologists can comprehend and record them only through their own idiosyncratic experience, we can say that, in this extreme sense, the bulk of anthropological data are biographical and collaborative. And, as we shall see later, it is our sense of our own lives that makes us believe we can easily understand the lives of others. Partly for this reason, we suspect, anthropological methods in general and life histories in particular have never been as readily accepted by the scientific community as they might have been.

Fieldwork was not always an integral part of anthropology. Even the greatest of the early anthropologists, people like Edward B. Tylor and James George Frazer, had virtually no first-hand contact with the various peoples they wrote about. They were "armchair anthropologists" who used the accounts of missionaries, travelers, and whomever to create their grand evolutionary theories. Even Franz Boas, often said to be the father of American anthropology, who undertook fieldwork with the Eskimo and the Kwakiutl and also understood the value of fieldwork, can hardly be said to have done fieldwork up to the standards set later by Bronislaw Malinowski and those who followed. Although Boas spent almost 30 months in the field between 1886 and 1931, his longest single period was in 1897, when he visited for only 3 months. He made some 13 trips in all. He did not live in the villages he visited nor can he be said to have been a participant observer in any meaningful sense of that term (Rohner 1969). The early students of Boas followed much the same procedure, visiting the reservations in the summers or on weekends, seldom staying with the people themselves, and trying to get through interviews with a few older informants what they could salvage of what were said to be "dying cultures." It was not unusual for anthropologists to actually list the names of their informants and the lists were characteristically brief. Little wonder, then, that an interest in life histories would emerge from this situation, and what began as personal reminiscences took on more and more importance as anthropology gradually attempted to become more systematic and scientific.

Rapport

The key to successful anthropological fieldwork and also to successful life-history taking is rapport. There are probably as many problems in establishing rapport as there are fieldworkers, fieldwork situations, and even individuals to be interviewed. Each ethnographer is a unique personality in a unique setting and must be able to adjust to the reactions his or her presence brings about in the subjects of study. Anthropologists must be able to cope with their own reactions as well. These stipulations apply equally whether the group to be studied is an isolated Amazon or New Guinea tribe with no previous contact with outsiders (a virtually unknown situation these days) or a highly urbanized and sophisticated subculture of the United States that has already been subjected to a seemingly endless variety of researchers, social workers, parole officers, Indian agents, and the like. Initial contact is always difficult, mainly because one must simultaneously be both cautious and bold, and also because, whether the fear is objectively valid or not, one usually fears that success or failure is linked to first impressions. A variety of techniques have been employed to help establish rapport. When working with remote nonliterate peoples it used to be helpful to offer inexpensive gifts in the form of beads, mirrors, knives, tinned foods, and so forth. More recently it has been found useful to take a tape recorder or polaroid camera, both of which offer dramatic and usually much appreciated diversions and quickly help to set up friendly relations.

In today's world, anthropologists and others are not always as welcome as they once were. It is frequently necessary to demonstrate that what you wish to do has some immediate or at least long-range relevance and practicality before you will even be permitted to begin. In the case of life histories it is even more difficult. Why, for example, should anyone wish to tell you the story of his or her life? Why, in particular, should illiterate individuals—living in a remote village with little or no understanding of scholarship, science, anthropology, or whatever—tell you about their "lives"? Why should anyone more knowledgeable or sophisticated tell you? We suspect the telling has rarely been for monetary reward alone (see Shaw 1980:230–231 for case material on the nonmonetary benefits perceived by his Aborigine informants). It appears, rather, that investigators convince their subjects that they have something important to tell—about their culture, about their handicap, about how their lives are changing, or the like. The inducement clearly involves a great deal of trust. We believe it is quite a remarkable comment on human nature that anthropologists have been able to establish such trust on the part of individuals all over the world.

Perhaps the most frequently used explanation for what one is doing
in the field, and one that does help immeasurably in gaining access, is
that you wish to learn the local language. As all fieldworkers should, if at
all possible, learn the language of those whose lives they are attempting
to understand, this claim is not false and it does act as a convenient way of
establishing relations and breaking down hostility and suspicion. It is
difficult to perceive someone as hostile or threatening when you can
laugh with the person at mistakes made when attempting to pronounce
your language's words and phrases for the first time.

Generally speaking, it has always been more difficult to establish
rapport with more acculturated groups such as most contemporary
American Indians and urban subcultures than with others, although
there are some glaring exceptions. Evans-Pritchard's well-known difficulties with the Nuer present a good case in point. The following
dialogue (1940:12–13) points up the problem:

I: Who are you?
Cuol: A man.
I: What is your name?
Cuol: Do you want to know my *name*?
I: Yes.
Cuol: You want to know *my* name?
I: Yes, you have come to visit me in my tent and I would like to know
who you are.
Cuol: All right. I am Cuol. What is your name?
I: My name is Pritchard.
Cuol: What is your father's name?
I: My father's name is also Pritchard.
Cuol: No, that cannot be true. You cannot have the same name as your
father.
I: It is the name of my lineage. What is the name of your lineage?
Cuol: Do you want to know the name of my lineage?
I: Yes.
Cuol: What will you do with it if I tell you? Will you take it to your
country?
I: I don't want to do anything with it. I just want to know it since I am
living at your camp.
Cuol: Oh well, we are Lou.
I: I did not ask you the name of your tribe. I know that. I am asking you
the name of your lineage.
Cuol: Why do you want to know the name of my lineage?
I: I don't want to know it.
Cuol: Then why do you ask me for it? Give me some tobacco.

In all cases success seems to be a question of caution, diplomacy, perseverance, and patience, along with repeated displays of good faith. Offers of money or other forms of remuneration, although often made as an incentive for performing some task, have little to do with establishing rapport as such and in most instances would be quite likely out of place. Most ethnographers who have done successful ethnographies or life histories deny that their informants were motivated by financial considerations but, of course, there almost always are indirect rewards of one kind or another. Quite often it is reported that the ethnographer was a friend or was adopted as a member of the family or clan.

It seems clear, however, that there is no substitute for an honest attempt to explain precisely who you are and what it is you wish to do, irrespective of the level of development of the people among whom you are working. Honesty is apparently universally understood at a level independent of the content of the particular communication.

The perceived role of the fieldworker is of great importance when it comes to rapport. That is, is he or she accepted and truly a participant observer, "one of them," so to speak, or is he or she the mysterious and powerful stranger of whom one should be suspicious and fearful? In most fieldwork situations one starts off as the latter, and only with time and great difficulty, if ever, becomes the former. (See, for example, our interview with Hilda Kuper in Chapter V.) In most cases the choice is not entirely up to the fieldworker. Early European fieldworkers in the New Guinea Highlands, for example, no matter how hard they might have tried, could never truly have become genuine members of the native community. This does not mean that they could not be accepted, adopted by someone, called by a kinship term, and even invited to participate in group activities; it means simply that the gulf separating the two cultures at that time was far too great for complete acceptance. The anthropologist's obvious visibility, status, and seemingly esoteric knowledge, coupled with the people's perfectly understandable fear, suspicion, and relative ignorance of the fieldworker's motives, was far too great to be entirely surmounted. This would have been true no matter how long the investigator stayed in the field or how fluent he or she might have been in the language. Adults socialized in one culture have difficulties of varying degrees in adapting to others, especially when the differences are pronounced. We do not mean to imply that the investigator's culture, whatever it is, is in its totality necessarily any better or worse than the one begin investigated, nor are we in any way suggesting that the investigator should attempt to impose reforms or display any disgust or repugnance; we merely wish to make clear that it is simply not realistic to expect too much and in some cases virtually impossible to "go native." The degree to which a fieldworker will be able to participate in another culture or understand another person's life will vary widely, depending first of all on the similarities of the two cultures and persons involved, and second upon temperaments, motivations, physical skills, and personal experiences. There have been instances recorded in which the anthropologist has gone to what would be considered extreme lengths to maintain rapport. Alan Holmberg's privations while working with the Sirionó are an excellent example. At times he found it necessary to subsist on palm cabbage, nuts, and fruit, and he often ate at night to avoid being disturbed by the perennially hungry people he followed on the march for game (1950). Colin Turnbull (1972) reports similar problems with food when he worked with the Ik of Uganda during a period of severe drought; and Napoleon Chagnon (1974) has reported at considerable length his difficuties in doing fieldwork with the Yąnomamö. While it is not usually necessary to go to the same lengths that Holmberg and Chagnon did, it must be understood that the fieldwork required of anthropologists demands great tolerance and dedication. Some of the best and most readable accounts of fieldwork by anthropologists, which offer much insight into what the experience is like, are *Return to Laughter* by Elenore Smith Bowen (1954), Kenneth E. Read's *The High Valley* (1965) and *Other Voices* (1980), Colin Turnbull's well-known *The Forest People* (1961), Paul Rabinow's *Reflections on Fieldwork in Morocco* (1977), and Paul Riesman's *Freedom in Fulani Social Life* (1977).

It is a truism in anthropology that fieldworkers should not identify too closely with their research subjects, as doing so destroys whatever objectivity there is in the anthropological enterprise. It is possible to be too close to your subjects and subject matter, even though you cannot completely cross the cultural boundaries, and thus be blinded to what is obvious to others who do not know the people so intimately. It has been reported that the early ethnographer, Frank Cushing, became so involved with the Zuñi that he eventually refused to publish any further accounts of them (Paul 1953:435). While this report has been shown to be more an anthropological myth than a reality, it is a myth which perhaps needed to be invented and passed on from one generation of anthropologists to another (Gronewold 1972). It is also possible, on the other hand, to be too aloof and thus to impair your work in the opposite direction. In this context it is important not to isolate yourself from everyday village life or from the lives of your informants. The amount of variation in fieldwork situations and interviewing habits is quite remarkable—but it is just as possible to be "too clean" and too careful in the field as it is to be "too dirty" and too casual.

There are some advantages in the role of stranger. As a friendly and objective outsider you can be called upon to arbitrate disputes, to offer opinions on subjects of mutual interest, to act as intermediary between the locals and some third party not so well known and trusted, to offer personal advice, and so on. Although it can be difficult it is important to avoid being categorized. Often the people with whom you are living and working have been exposed to only a limited number of outsiders and know them only as missionaries, planters, traders, government workers, or other such types. As in all cases of labeling, if you are categorized among these your work will necessarily suffer. Even worse, needless to say, especially in recent years, is the danger of being seen as the agent of a foreign power, a spy, or an intelligence agent. To establish your role as an anthropologist takes time. There is simply no substitute for honesty, patience, tolerance, fairness, and good humor, come what may.

It is obvious that the taking of an adequate and reliable life history involves a degree of intimacy with the informant, and a knowledge of the community as well, that comes only with exceptionally good rapport. For this reason it is usually not advisable to attempt a life history until one has known the person and/or been in the field for some reasonable period of time. The attention devoted to one or few individuals, or the rewards offered, can create envy and resentment in others. For a male anthropologist, working with female informants can be particularly difficult, and only after coming to know the people and the customs well is one prepared to anticipate and handle the problems that inevitably arise. Female anthropologists may likewise find that they are barred from having contact with potential informants who are male or from discussing certain topics with them. Indeed, in certain situations the fieldworker may well come to the conclusion that attempting life histories is not worth the cost in time or in rapport, and this seems to have been the case in certain areas of the world such as the New Guinea Highlands. This situation is unfortunate and the ethnographic materials from New Guinea suffer as a result of it.

There are other reasons for waiting, too, before attempting intensive life-history work with one or few informants. Quite often there are village, clan, or other political factions, and it does not pay to become quickly identified with any one of them and thus alienated from the others. The first few months of fieldwork are difficult; you may not yet be sensitive to myriad cues sent out by the strange people you are with nor are you familiar with the hierarchy of power and influence. There are many other things to do besides talking life histories, and it is well to do them first; these include less value-laden or conflict-laden activities such as mapping gardens, counting livestock, diagramming villages, and so on.

For useful discussions of participant observation see: "The Participant Observer Technique in Small Communities (Florence Kluckhohn 1940), "The Methodology of Participant Observation" and "The New Empiricists: The Participant Observer and Phenomenologist" (Bruyn 1970a, 1970b), and "Participant Observation as Role and Method in Behavioral Research" (Pearsall 1970). See also *Stress and Response in Fieldwork* (Henry and Saberwal 1969), *Doing Fieldwork: Warnings and Advice* (Wax 1971), and *People Studying People* (Georges and Jones 1980).

Language

Although it had long been recognized that the anthropological fieldworker should learn the local language if possible (Lowie 1940), it was not until Malinowski's unprecedented ethnographic achievement with the Trobriand Islanders (1922) that the crucial significance of knowing the language was brought clearly into focus. Since Malinowski's high standards were established, it has become commonplace for most fieldworkers to try to emulate him in this respect, but they have done so with widely differing degrees of success. Obviously not everyone has the same facility for learning languages, not all languages are as easy to learn as others, and not all fieldworkers have the same length of time to spend learning the language as did Malinowski. This situation has stimulated some scholars in the past to make rather exaggerated claims as to their language skills in the field. Margaret Mead wrote an article in 1939 in which she made clear the distinction between learning and using the native language. She pointed out that it was not necessary to completely learn the language in order to do competent fieldwork, and that different levels of language skills would suffice for different tasks. For example, if one is investigating swidden agriculture it is not quite as critical to learn the language as it is if one is researching native religion, magic, or conceptions of the universe and the good life. Furthermore, as would be expected, a great deal depends upon what the contact language is and how fluent any of the subjects are in it. That is, if the contact language is English, the anthropologist speaks English, and a substantial number of informants speak English, there are no grave problems in communication. If the contact language is Dutch, the investigator speaks English, and only one or two natives speak Dutch, it obviously is crucial for the investigator to learn the native language. Clearly, if doing an in-depth life history is the goal, and you are attempting to get at someone's subjective meanings, interpretations, perceptions, and understandings, you should by all means be fluent in your subject's language and even sensitive to the finest of nuances. This need involves a level of understanding not often achieved in published life histories and, although many good life histories have been produced through interpreters and translations, it remains an ideal to be approximated as closely as possible.

In some cases a *lingua franca* is available, as in Melanesia where Pidgin English is widely spoken. Pidgin English, contrary to what many believe, is a bona fide language (Murphy 1959; Mihalic 1971), and has in fact become the official language of Papua New Guinea. Although it has a limited vocabulary, it can be quite effective for most purposes. What generally happens when doing fieldwork in Pidgin is that after a time the investigator will mix many native words, especially nouns, with the Pidgin: these aid measurably in communication with informants. Also, if one is fortunate enough to find a good interpreter to work with for an extended period of time, their common fund of experience makes it possible to communicate at a much higher level of understanding than would otherwise be the case. Even so, it is usually difficult to communicate in Pidgin languages at a highly abstract level, and it is obvious that much more can be accomplished with fluency in the subject's language.

The problem of interpretation, like all aspects of fieldwork, depends upon the location, the particular circumstances, the amount of foreign contact, and other related factors. In some areas of New Guinea, although they are by now getting exceedingly rare, there are few if any Pidgin speakers, whereas in others virtually everyone speaks it.

Even assuming that an interpreter of ideal qualifications can be found, it does not follow that adequate life histories will be forthcoming. Not all concepts and words can be readily translated, first of all, and satisfactory translation also demands that the translator understand fully the investigator's motives, which cannot always be assumed, especially when working with relatively isolated nonliterates.

There are other problems involved in working through an interpreter. It is sometimes difficult to talk to a third party about certain areas of human behavior such as sexuality, personal habits, family matters, or questions that may involve reasons for secrecy. Thus although an informant may be willing to tell you how many pigs he has, he may not be willing to divulge such information to a native interpreter. This kind of problem becomes even more serious and sometimes almost impossible when trying to work with an informant of the same sex through an interpreter of the opposite sex. A native male, for example, may refuse even to ask a question relating to menstruation, childbirth, intercourse, or similar topics. Here again, however, one must be careful not to be ethnocentric. Langness found when working with one New Guinea woman that he simply could not predict with any degree of accuracy what she would discuss and what she would not discuss. The same thing proved to be true of the interpreter he was using, and thus the problems were mainly due to his own inhibitions rather than to those of the people with whom he was working. Furthermore, the problems had not only to do with his relative ignorance of the culture but also, as it turned out, with the unique circumstances which motivated the two natives to work for him in the first place.

If one has some grasp of the native language, even if far from fluent, it is possible to follow an interpretation with at least some idea of what is transpiring and how well the interpreter is sticking to the facts. A check can also be made at selected points at other times by using different interpreters and repeating questions. If the subject knows a few words of the contact language, a more direct check can be made of certain salient points as well. Certainly one should not refrain from attempting a life history because of the necessity of working through an interpreter, at least not without first trying.

For an unusual and particularly instructive account of problems involved in translation we refer you to the book *Faithful Echo* by Robert B. Ekvall (1960), a missionary turned anthropologist who was called upon to act as English-Chinese interpreter at Panmunjom and Geneva. While this book does not deal specifically with the ethnographic field situation, many of the pitfalls of translation are insightfully exposed.

Interviewing

The interview is probably the most crucial single act anthropologists in the field engage in, and much of their success depends upon how skillful and perceptive they are in the interview situation. Interviewing means, essentially, the gathering of data through direct or indirect questioning. The general nature of the interview is the same in all fields in which it is featured as a technique, but there are some special problems in anthropological interviewing. Not the least of these are the problems of rapport and language already mentioned. The significance of the interview situation varies widely from person to person, but it also varies cross-culturally. Even the amount of information a person will volunteer varies widely and some people talk much more freely than others. Kaplan has reported extremely wide variation in the amount of responses given to projective test cards (1961:246) and we know from our own experience that the same is true for interviewing in general. Some New Guinea Highlanders, for example, have been known to seldom answer with more than a barely audible yes or no, while some American Indians we have worked with would talk almost uninterruptedly for hours.

The significance attached to an interview by someone who is illiterate and does not comprehend the aims of science or data collection is obviously much different from that of a more sophisticated urban dweller being interviewed for a job. The aim of the illiterate may often be to just get it over with as quickly as possible so as to get back to more understandable pursuits such as gardening or hunting. Similarly, the social role assigned to the interviewer makes a great difference, and thus the information given can vary greatly from situation to situation. When Langness worked in the New Guinea Highlands, for example, people often distorted the truth when talking to patrol officers, missionaries, and others. The motives for these falsehoods were usually not difficult to understand as the people had a tendency to tell strangers what they thought they would like to hear; they did not like having to tell how many pigs or other possessions they had, that they had neglected something they should have done, and so on. Here anthropologists have a tremendous advantage because they are constantly present and interacting with the people over a relatively long period. This association greatly increases the reliability and the validity of the information in both ethnography and life-history taking. (For a review of techniques to enhance the reliability, validity, and comparability of life histories, see Frank 1980a: 163–170.) It is difficult to sustain a web of falsehoods over a long period and anthropologists also have the advantage of often being able to match up statements and observations on the spot. When this cannot be done they can use repeated interviews with the same informant over an extended period, constantly checking and rechecking. They can also check an interview with one person against another interviewee and thus uncover inconsistencies and fabrications. Different informants often give quite different accounts of the same thing. If it is impossible to assess objectively which account is the correct one, either through observation or consensus, the anthropologist should specify that there were such differences of opinion. Here the personal qualities of the informant become very important and this, again, indicates the necessity of knowing the people well. It should be apparent that a life history based upon many hours spent with the same individual and upon other information about the person gathered from those who know him or her is a much more reliable and valid account than an abbreviated version acquired through questionnaires, surveys, or other short-term techniques.

A related matter here is the fact that informants, especially those who become candidates for a life history, are not selected purely fortuitously. On the other hand, marginal individuals, deviants, and those who are not as actively participating in daily tasks are often the most likely to present themselves to the fieldworker. These are the individuals with the most time to spend watching the anthropologist at work and following him or her around. Sometimes such persons can be exceptionally good subjects for life histories, particularly if deviance is a particular interest, but one needs to be wary of getting an overly idiosyncratic view of the culture and of other people. On the other hand, the anthropologist doubtless has his or her own idiosyncrasies, peculiarities, or interests that lead to the selection of one informant over another. Clearly the selection process, when it comes to an intensive life history, involves two parties, and both come with their own desires and needs, some of which are unconscious. It is absolutely crucial, then, when attempting a life history, to understand your own needs and motives and how they influence and intertwine with what you are attempting.

Whether doing ordinary fieldwork interviewing or more intensive life-history interviewing, the interviews should be combined if possible with direct observations of behavior. If, for example, you wish information about a marriage, an illness, or whatever, the most satisfactory situation is to observe the event in progress and interview the subject or subjects simultaneously. If you wish to truly understand someone's life, or at least the person's account of the life, it is necessary to participate in it, to accompany informants while they pursue their ordinary activities, and to be available for extraordinary events as well. There is a drawback in this approach, of course, as the presence of the investigator may frequently change the behavior of the subject. He or she may feel laughed at, may be inhibited for other reasons from acting naturally, or may actually modify personal behavior to accommodate the investigator. In spite of this problem of reactivity, however, anthropologists and other social scientists have been able to record some unusual and exceptionally personal kinds of data. Indeed, it is a remarkable fact of human behavior that anthropologists have been able to travel to virtually every type of culture known, establish rapport, and accumulate data on even the most private and sensitive areas of life.

The interview does give some information that cannot be checked by observation. Beliefs about the supernatural, traditions, myths, dreams, and so forth, although they may be reflected in certain forms of behavior, really exist only in the minds of the actors. Likewise, when emotions and judgments are involved there can be no subtitute for the in-depth interview. When the investigator is trying to assess motivations, judgments, values, attitudes, and emotions, the interview is the most direct and satisfactory method. When emotions or matters of morality are involved it is often difficult to get informants to respond at all. In situations such as these it often helps to stimulate informants by a more aggressive line of questioning or, conversely, a more indirect mode. Interviewing is importantly an art, but one that can be readily improved through practice and experience.

Perhaps it is unfortunate, but as Beals has pointed out: "The student of culture cannot ignore the objective situation, but it is the subjective view that constitutes his distinctive concern" (1953:442). For this very reason it is important to take intensive life histories and to be sensitive to the meanings and nuances of behavior in the interview situation. Informants will often betray by a sign or gesture or by an expression that they do not really mean what they say, or that if they do mean it something further is involved. It is very dangerous to accept and repeat verbal statements without specifying, at least in your own mind, the context in which you acquired the information. A female informant in New Guinea reported to Langness, for example, that she and everyone else disapproved of the fact that another woman was having an illegitimate child. Her demeanor, however, indicated a contrary attitude. Further questioning brought out that although she was repeating what can be considered the moral rule for such behavior, she and the other woman in fact believed it was good for the woman to have asserted herself and to have "put one over" on the men, so to speak. With respect to situations similar to this we can see why it is desirable for the anthropologist to have some knowledge of the psychiatric interview. What Harry Stack Sullivan has written of this is just as pertinent to the anthropologist as to the psychiatrist:

> The psychiatrist cannot stand off to one side and apply his sense organs, however they may be refined by the use of apparatus, to noticing what someone else does, without becoming personally implicated in the operation. His principal instrument of observation is his self— his personality, him as a person. The processes and the changes in processes that make up the data which can be subjected to scientific study occur, not in the subject person nor in the observer, but in the situation which is created between the observer and his subject. (1954:3)

It is most unfortunate that anthropologists who have successfully collected life histories have not often given much information about what actually transpired in their interview situations and what their relationship to their informants was. As was mentioned previously, virtually without exception anthropological biographers have denied giving material remuneration to their informants, but even so they often have not discussed their relationship beyond the fact that they were "friends" or adopted kin. There clearly are in the anthropologist-informant relationship problems of transference, countertransference, identification, and other transpersonal phenomena. These problems have seldom been either described or analyzed. A knowledge of these phenomena on the part of the anthropologist, and further serious attempts to deal with them, as in the recent works of Vincent Crapanzano (1980), Jean-Paul Dumont (1978), Paul Rabinow (1977), and Paul Riesman (1977), would be most welcome.

Although there are points of similarity, an anthropological interview is not the same as a psychiatric interview. The relationship between patient and therapist is well defined, the aims of both participants are more or less clear, and the interview is almost always private and takes place in essentially the same circumstances each time. In the field, however, the anthropologist must conduct interviews when the opportunity arises. They may take place in a crowd. They may have continual interruptions by children or others. It may be a more formal interview in the anthropologist's home. It could well be an informal interview that arises as you are walking or sitting with someone. The differences not only affect the conduct of the interview and the recording of it but also can substantially affect the content as well. It is well established in therapy that the therapist's couch allows people to relax and to free associate more easily than they would otherwise. Other situations help to elicit different types of information. We know of one case in which a man preferred to be interviewed while driving his car, as he claimed to be much less defensive and inhibited while doing so. And obviously people do not tend to reveal their innermost thoughts and feelings in a crowd or where they fear being overheard. It is possible to do group interviewing, and in most situations the participants stimulate each other in a very productive way. Beals (1953:44) reports some striking cross-cultural diversity, however, and there are people who, under some circumstances, do not communicate well in groups. There are obvious advantages to interviewing people alone. An adult may become quite careful in the presence of a child or vice versa. A man may be inhibited in the presence of a woman. Often women defer to men or are preempted by them in conversation or in group situations where both sexes are present (Collins 1980). Women and children, in New Guinea at least, are very careful of what they say in the presence of men. A rather striking example of this among the Bena involves the denial by adults that children dream. When Langness first learned of this he queried some children nearby, who all denied dreaming. Later, when talking with children alone, they would sometimes recount their dreams to him and they made it clear that adults laughed at them and teased them if

they said anything about their dreams. There is much more to this than
one might suspect—dreams are important to the Bena, are regarded as
omens, and can be very disturbing. It is not that Bena children do not
dream but rather that their dreams are regarded as too trivial to be
acknowledged.

Interviews can be either directed or nondirected. That is, the
interviewer may have a particular topic in mind and thus keep an
informant constantly on it, bringing the conversation back to it
whenever the informant begins to stray. This type of interview is
probably best employed in the latter stages of taking a life history, as it is
wise to encourage spontaneity at first. One of the advantages of
nondirective or open-ended interviewing is precisely that it does
encourage spontaneity. This enables you to learn what the subjects
themselves regard as important—or at least what they think it is
important to tell the interviewer. Spontaneity, moreover, enables you to
learn how the informants conceptualize and think about their own
lives—the so-called "emic" view that anthropologists have emphasized
at least from the early 1900s (Langness 1974). As most biographical
materials have been presented in chronological form there is a strong
tendency to think that all people necessarily conceive their life to be a
natural chronology of events from birth to death. We know this is just
not so and that how different people perceive their lives is an interesting
and important topic in its own right, which we will discuss in Chapter IV.

Some people tend to arrange their lives according to what they
perceive as the most important single aspect—work, for example.
Others focus on motherhood, professional identity, or other such
things. While many do see their lives as chronological, others do not.
One man of whom we know, for example, conceives of his life as a series
of linked bubbles, each one of which refers to some significant event or
period; yet they do not represent equal units of time. Thus, for example,
the period he spent in the Armed Forces, although of relatively brief
duration when compared with his total life span, looms dispropor-
tionately large as he relates the story of his life. The period of his
childhood, from infancy to high school, although much longer, is
treated as mostly insignificant.

Some people tend to be very much oriented toward the past, some to
the present or future. One life history collected by Langness is
characterized by the subject's preoccupation with what his life "might

have been" had it not been disrupted by culture contact. The New Guinea Highlanders with whom Langness worked do not spontaneously tell their life stories in chronological order and in fact seem to have difficulty recounting their lives chronologically when asked. Nondirective interviewing of New Guinea men very often results in stories of warfare and raiding beginning when the person was an adolescent or a young adult. Childhood tends to be regarded as too unimportant to be mentioned and warfare was an important focus of male activity.

While nondirective interviewing is desirable, it is usually not possible to depend entirely on such an approach as it can result in much too narrow a focus. In order to insure as complete an account as possible it is desirable to jot down questions as they come to you, keep an outline of the materials you already have, and then turn eventually to more directed interviews.

The interview being so crucial to anthropological research, students should prepare themselves for it, if possible, by taking practical course work in interviewing; they should also practice interviewing with a number of informants. Many good works on interviewing are available and time spent with them and in practice will pay off handsomely in the field. Sullivan's *The Psychiatric Interview* (1954) is highly recommended. For a more thorough and fundamental discussion of behavioral-science methods that bears directly upon problems of transference and the relation of investigators to their subjects and work, see George Devereux's important work *From Anxiety to Method in the Behavioral Sciences* (1967). For an account of some cultural aspects of transference see Spiegel (1959). A general treatment of interviewing is *Interviewing: Its Forms and Functions* (Richardson, Dohrenwend, and Klein 1965). See also Cannell and Kahn (1953) and Maccoby and Maccoby (1954). For still-useful discussions of anthropological interviewing see Nadel (1939) and Paul (1953). For an account of interviewing as a scientific procedure see Hyman (1951). Nondirective interviewing has been discussed by Rogers (1945) and by Dohrenwend and Richardson (1963). The focused interview has been treated at some length in a book of that name by Merton, Fiske, and Kendall (1956). Depth interviewing has been discussed by Gorden (1956) and by Link (1943). For a useful discussion of cross-class interviewing see Strauss and Schatzman (1960), and see Lerner (1956) for an example of cross-cultural interviewing. A recent book that offers a step-by-step, how-to-do-it approach to anthropological interviewing is *The Ethnographic Interview* (1979) by James P. Spradley. See also Michael Agar's (1980) guide to fieldwork.

Reliability and Sampling

Anthropologists in general, and those in particular who have engaged in life-history work, are often criticized for the unreliability of their data and for inadequate sampling. How do you know that what your informants tell you is correct?

In fieldwork in general, and in taking life histories, all other things being equal, the longer the anthropologist has been in the field or with the person the greater is the likelihood that the data will be reliable. Although there are different ways of checking the verbal information received, probably the best test of reliability is simply the ability to predict accurately what people will do in a given situation and to understand what is happening. Fieldworkers whose information is reliable will be able to get around comfortably in the culture, to avoid errors and *faux pas*, and to elicit predictable responses from the individuals they interact with. That is to say, people will do what the fieldworker, on the basis of the data, thinks they will do. When the expected occurs it confirms the working hypotheses about the culture or the person which the investigator is constantly formulating and revising. When a predictable response does not occur, either the previous information was unreliable, or there are previously unknown conditions operating which will need to be considered.

There are three techniques for checking the reliability of anthropological data as they are accumulated in the field. The first of these is observation. If, for example, you have never seen a funeral but have had one described to you, and then you do witness one, you can check your description against what actually occurs. Our own experience in New Guinea and with American Indians indicates that verbal descriptions are usually fairly accurate but that many details are simply omitted. The reason is not dishonesty on the part of informants but simply that it is difficult to give a detailed account of this kind from memory. The observation of the event not only confirms the reliability or unreliability of previous information but it fills in details and should moreover make sense.

Another way of assessing the reliability of information is to check the account of one informant against that of another. If you are attending a ceremony and are told that a particular act of magic is performed to "make the pigs grow," it makes sense for you to move among the crowd asking several people the same question. When doing this, you might receive somewhat different answers from different people. If so, you must take into account the age and sex of the informants, their social position, their relationship to participants in the ritual, and so on. Sometimes, for example, children and adults will give different explanations, usually because the children have not yet accumulated as much knowledge about things as have the older people. The consistency of response is an index of reliability.

A third way, and one that is particularly relevant to the life history, is to ask the same questions of the same informant repeatedly over a long period of time. It is not necessary to be impolite or skeptical, but it pays to repeat questions and to ask the same questions in different ways. You can often do this by simply pleading your own ignorance. You might say, for example, "I know we discussed this before but I still don't feel I understand it," or "Your customs are difficult for one to understand. Tell me once more about such-and-such."

It is not necessary, of course, to accept an informant's statement as the truth about some action or event. As Becker (1970:192) has pointed out, it is possible to use the statement as evidence *about* an action or event. To do this you must ask yourself if the person has reason to conceal the truth. You must evaluate whether or not he or she actually saw the event in question. Does the person have strong feelings about any of the participants that would lead him or her to distort or fabricate? What position did he or she play in the event or action and how would that have affected the recounting of it? And so on. And even if the statement can be shown to be defective, it can still be used as a different kind of information that provides evidence for a different kind of conclusion. Although there are obvious problems of reliability in life-history work there is no reason to suppose these are intrinsically more difficult than problems in most social-science research, except insofar as rapport, language, and other factors of the cross-cultural situation constitute special problems that anthropologists have had to deal with more than others.

Anthropologists have often been criticized on the grounds of inadequate sampling and, in many cases, rightly so. In the early days of ethnographic research little or no attention was paid to the question of sampling. Ethnographers simply interviewed whomever they found who could tell them what they wanted to know. Similarly, they took life histories wherever they found them although sometimes, like Radin, they may have tried to find "a representative middle-aged individual."

Naturally if your goal is to use life histories to learn about culture or about something like "modal personality" or "national character," you should strive to get a number of them drawn as randomly as possible from the group you are interested in. It is important to get an adequate sampling of age, sex, and social position. And it is also important that you get similar information of the kind you require from each informant. If, for example, there is a belief in ghosts, you should know how women feel about them as well as men, how children perceive them as well as adults, and what the full range of variation is within the community. While it is true that certain categories of information are associated predominantly with one category of person, menstruation with women or warfare most often with men, for example, it is equally important to learn what, if anything, men know about menstruation or women about warfare. The ideal situation is one in which identical questions have been asked of a completely representative sample of the population. The sum total gathered from this procedure would be a collection of detailed life histories which, from among the idiosyncrasies of individuals, one could also draw similar materials on the feelings, attitudes, knowledge, and beliefs of the sample on the broadest range of culture. In practice this completeness is very difficult to obtain. It is all too easy to settle down in the field with one major informant or interpreter and base your work mainly on the reports of that one person. Not all people in a culture are as easy to work with as others, and not all are willing to give their time to an anthropologist. A comfortable relationship with one or few informants is easier than the discomfort of working with those persons you do not like or trying constantly to form new relationships. Even if you cannot obtain the ideal it is important to work with as large a number of informants as feasible and with as adequate a sample as possible. Above all, it is always essential to specify why and how a particular informant was chosen and to let your readers know what kinds of inferences and generalizations they may make on the basis of that single case.

Naturally, if your interest is in a particular individual, sampling is irrelevant. Life histories have often been done on deviants or on particularly interesting individuals who were leaders or were unusual in some other way. (See, for example, Kennedy 1977; Langness *In press*; Wilson 1974) Such accounts can tell us a great deal about culture even though the person is not truly representative. Indeed, Margaret Mead has argued that *any* individual, with certain qualifications, can be taken as representative of a culture in some sense:

> Any member of a group, provided that his position within that group is properly specified, is a perfect sample of the group wide pattern on which he is acting as an informant. So a twenty-one-year old boy born of Chinese-American parents in a small upstate New York town who has just graduated *summa cum laude* from Harvard and a tenth-generation Boston-born deaf mute of United Kingdom stock are equally perfect examples of American national character, provided that their individual position and individual characteristics are taken fully into account. (1953:648)

Unfortunately, to be able to specify precisely what any individual's position within the culture is, and to also specify their individual characteristics, involves a previous and very thorough knowledge of both the culture and the individual that almost begs the question. Nonetheless, there is something to Mead's claim and, as all individuals are necessarily members of a culture and a society, information about them as individuals must also give us information about others.

Supplemental Data

All data on a given individual are a part of his or her life history. We wish to distinguish here, however, between the simple questioning and verbal exchange that goes on in the two-party interview and information from other sources. "Other sources" means such things as reports about the individual from others, psychological testing, a medical history if one is available, or any other kind of information that one might obtain.

Projective testing, although no substitute for an intensive life history, can be a valuable adjunct to the life history, particularly when comparisons with other individuals are intended. Psychological tests, other than those of the "projective" variety, have not been popular with anthropologists mainly because they have proven to be "culture bound." The projective tests (mainly the Rorschach, Thematic Apperception Test, Free Drawings, Doll Play, and the Bender Gestalt), being usually a series of standardized stimulus objects, offer more comparable results than does the nonstandardized interview. A further advantage of testing is that it allows anthropologists to get at least some personality data on a larger number of individuals than they would otherwise be able to interview in the relatively short amount of time usually allotted to fieldwork. The tests are short, fairly easy to administer, and can be analyzed by persons other than the fieldworker. One must be cautious, however, not to take this procedure for more than it is actually worth. The tests, even the best of them, do not measure personality-as-a-whole. They are of very limited utility for personality assessment apart from intensive life-history data from other sources. Kaplan has written of this:

> The first assumption, for example, that the projective test samples adequately the personality processes of the individual in whom one is interested, is an extremely hazardous one. There is ample reason to believe from intensive studies of individuals using many techniques, or from studies of successive administrations of a single test, that the data obtained from a single test is little more than a fragment which may on occasion have some central importance but which at best is only part of the story of personality. (1961:238)

Another problem has to do with the fact that such tests can be seriously loaded toward eliciting pathology, not surprising perhaps when it is remembered that projective tests were developed for working with persons having personality problems and mental illnesses. In any case they do tend to produce themes such as loneliness, unhappiness, conflict, frustration, inadequacy, and so on. The Thematic Apperception Test is particularly noted for this. Consider what Caroline Preston, a psychologist with many years of experience in the field of psychological testing, writes in the following paper she did on the Eskimo:

> How often in using these particular T.A.T. cards I have had the experience with subjects in our own culture asking me plaintively, 'Don't you have any happy pictures?' Certainly there cards are designed to militate against superficial or innocuous fantasy material in the story responses . . . however, I am surprised at the frequency with which our people are able to ignore or deny the potentialities for tragedy in their story responses. (1964:392)

In an attempt to clarify her Eskimo findings, Preston constructed a four-fold typology that permitted her to rate an "unhappy" situation with either "happy" or "unhappy" feelings and a "happy" situation similarly. The particular classifications of "happy" and "unhappy" were suggested by the Eskimo test results themselves. This typology is a worthwhile attempt to compensate for the loading toward pathology. Even after constructing it, however, Preston found that the "tragic" stories outnumber "innocuous" two to one, and "unhappy" feelings outnumber "happy" feelings by approximately the same proportion. Recognizing the absence of any norms with which to compare her results, Preston speculates that the result may be due to: (1) Eskimo attitudes toward whites; (2) depression brought about by the practical realities of Eskimo life, or by a related factor; (3) fatalism in Eskimo personality. Whereas any or all of these interpretations may prove to be correct, as Preston notes, one cannot escape the fact of the overwhelming bias toward pathology.

When you couple the "unhappy" nature of the stimulus cards in the case of the T.A.T. with the additional possibility of scoring bias, the situation appears even worse. That is, there is a tendency to score certain responses involving sexuality and aggression as pathological, or at least undesirable, whereas in another cultural context these responses may have quite a different meaning. Thus we would tend to see a group of people less inhibited about these matters than we are in an even more unrealistic pathological light, albeit when responding in a healthy, honest, and straightforward manner.

For the many other problems involved, which are far too extensive to go into here, see David Spain's thorough revision of the Kaplan chapter cited above (1972). The use of projective tests by anthropologists has fallen off drastically since the 1960s, partly because of the many problems inherent in their use, and partly because of changing interests within the professions of anthropology and psychology. As the concept of personality has fallen more and more into disfavor, so have the variety of projective tests that were designed to assess personality attributes (Shweder 1979). Ironically perhaps, the use of detailed life histories fell off in the medical profession and among psychologists even earlier. This change has been reported by Burton and Harris, who attribute it to the influence of "Rogerian, Sullivanian, and other post-Freudian points of view," in which "genetic reconstructions and overall conceptualizations of a life history are less often attempted" (1955:xi). A similar neglect has been pointed out for general medicine by Blumer (1949:3), who attributes it to an increase in the number of diagnostic aids available, such as x-ray, electrocardiograms, electroencephalograms, and so on.

In spite of the many formidable problems, projective testing of some kind can be useful and can elicit information you might not otherwise obtain. For example, when Langness administered a T.A.T. to an older man in the New Guinea Highlands, the subject suddenly and most unexpectedly launched into a detailed description of how to butcher and cook a human body. While such a question might well be asked by an investigator working with people who were known to have been cannibals, it also might well have been overlooked or even avoided as a direct question. Certainly many of the objections to the use of projective tests to elicit comparative materials do not apply to their use in individual life-history work where they can lead to many useful insights and new directions.

When taking life-history data, one should always strive to get as much information as possible from persons other than the subject. In this way it is possible to pick up discrepancies between individuals' conceptions of themselves and the conceptions others have of them. It also usually enables the researcher to obtain information concerning topics about which they might be reticent, especially if something of a shameful or distasteful nature has occurred in the subject's life. One man Langness worked with for some time, for example, never told him that he had refused to be initiated, a fact of singular importance in his life and a source of constant embarrassment to him. When Langness finally learned of it from others he managed to get some of the informant's feeling about it even though he still could not talk freely about it. Individuals who are giving their life histories do tend to leave out such things and they also distort them. A Clallam informant Langness worked with, a hunchback since birth, insisted repeatedly that he had been born normal and had fallen from a wagon onto a stump when three years of age. This story helped him cope with intense feelings of inferiority, and he refused to give it up even when faced with the contradictory statements of others who had known him since birth (Langness *In press*). It pays to be discrete in this kind of inquiry, however, and generally speaking, when someone else tells you something about a person you should think carefully before repeating it to the person involved. In addition to finding out from others about someone, if at all possible, it pays to keep a daily record of what the person does, and also to keep notes about your feelings toward the subject, for they can easily color the way you interpret and present your materials.

The genealogical method (Rivers 1910) is a useful way of collecting information about an individual. Here again it pays to go into as much depth and to do as much probing as possible. It is one thing to sit down with informants and record the kinship terms they use for various categories of kin but quite another to elicit their real feelings and attitudes toward these kin. Informants are usually loath to admit that although they should love an elder brother, for instance, they actually despise him. Likewise, kinship terms involve certain rights and obligations, and a person does not always willingly admit to having failed in meeting such obligations. Anthropologists have often been criticized by others for painting too rosy a picture of the "primitive world" and this is, in part at least, a fair criticism. The anthropologist interviews informants, collects the kinship terms, and everyone really does turn out to be a mother or father or brother or sister to everyone else. The terms imply certain kinds of behavior, usually of a benevolent character, and the real emotions and attitudes are often hidden behind a screen of defenses. The only possible attempt to penetrate these defenses is to do extensive in-depth and clinical interviewing, resulting in a correspondingly intensive life history.

All kinds of data are valuable for the life history. Photographs, taken in as many situations as possible, are an invaluable aid, for once you have left the field your memory fades rapidly. Tape recordings are also helpful. Items manufactured by the individual can be useful, especially if you have others to compare them with, as they can reveal personality quirks or consistencies. An inventory of the person's household can be useful, as well as accurate descriptions or maps of the location of houses and gardens, or both, and so forth. If you are fortunate enough to obtain materials in the form of a medical or prison record, you can put them to good use. If you know the individual lived in another area for a time it pays, if at all feasible, to visit there and interview people who knew him or her under the different circumstances. When people are well known outside their own group, it is valuable to get the impressions of "outsiders" who know of them.

Note Taking and Recording

The faithful recording of useful fieldnotes, the unglamorous but absolutely essential backbone of anthropology, is probably the most difficult part of life-history taking. It demands great dedication and much discipline to write or type up notes that can often run to pages and pages daily over an extended time.

The taking of notes is a very idiosyncratic procedure. There is a story of an anthropologist who wrote very large on foolscap paper and who, at the end of his fieldwork, had a ton of notes to ship home! Others prefer more modest notes, typewritten or handwritten, on cards, in notebooks, or even on scraps of paper. It probably makes little difference just how one actually records information provided it can be easily retrieved and worked with later, but certain obvious facts of recording are worth reviewing. It is important for the sake of reliability and completeness of record to write notes as soon as possible. Preferably, one should take notes during the interview. This is not always possible either because of the awkward physical situation anthropologists often find themselves in, or because they or their informants are disturbed by note taking. If it is not possible to write or type notes during the interview, it is important to pause often during the day to write things down. Too long an interview, or too long an interval between interview and recording, can cause much consternation when it comes to accurate and detailed recall. As nearly as we can determine from the literature, most anthropological fieldworkers have had no trouble with on-the-spot note taking and the inhibition is more usually of the anthropologist's own making, though there are exceptions.

The retrieval of information from field notes has been a topic of much discussion among anthropologists, although virtually nothing has been written about it. Some anthropologists use the *Outline of Cultural Materials* (Murdock et al. 1971) as a guide to coding their notes. Still others have relied on the less thorough but still useful *Notes and Queries on Anthropology*, which first came out in 1874 and has been republished and revised ever since (Royal Anthropological Institute 1954). Quite likely, most fieldworkers make up their own system of indexing as they go along, concentrating only on a relatively few categories they are specifically interested in. It is this personal and idiosyncratic quality of fieldnotes that has made most anthropologists reluctant to make their notes public. But whatever system individual fieldworkers devise, it is an absolute necessity that there be *some* system, and that it will work well enough to permit them to use their materials once they are out of the field and away from the immediate situation. For some of the problems involved in coding ethnographic data see the chapter by LeBar in *A Handbook of Method in Cultural Anthropology* (Naroll and Cohen 1970).

It is also important to keep a detailed record of the context of the interview. Were you told something, for instance, in an "unguarded moment" (Langness 1970) or in a relaxed or formal atmosphere? Did you find it necessary to probe for the information or was it volunteered? Was it in the context of a group discussion or one-to-one? Who was present? It also pays to jot down your own impressions as to what was going on, how people appeared to you at that time, and so forth. Any additional detail can be valuable later when going over your notes and trying to remember what it was like at the time and what it all meant. It can be most helpful to keep a diary or daily record in which you record your own feelings, fluctuations in mood, mental condition, the events of the day in chronological order, and anything else that strikes you as significant.

Finally, there are obvious reasons for taking notes in duplicate and mailing one copy home where it will be safe. Many anthropologists have had their notes stolen or have lost them en route from the field. There is always danger of fire or some natural calamity, and it pays to be very careful with the product of a year or more of very difficult and frustrating work. It is possible to buy notebooks with dual pages and carbon inserts and the fieldworker is well advised to do so.

In the earliest days of fieldwork the only way data could be recorded was in written fieldnotes, sketches, or paintings. Today anthropologists increasingly employ audio and video recording, and still and motion-picture photography. The earliest and still probably most important attempt to use photography as an aid in fieldwork is *Balinese Character: A Photographic Analysis* by Gregory Bateson and Margaret Mead (1942). A discussion of this, along with new materials and a more general discussion of fieldwork techniques, can be found in "The Art and Technology of Field Work" (Mead 1970). For a general discussion of photography as a research method see John Collier's *Visual Anthropology: Photography as a Research Method* (1967) and *Ethnographic Film* by Karl Heider (1976). See also *Principles of Visual Anthropology* (Hockings 1975). Jay Ruby has discussed specifically the problems of attempting to film a life history (1977).

Personality

It has often been suggested that anthropological fieldworkers should undergo psychoanalysis before going into the field. The purpose of such an analysis is, of course, to give investigators insight into their own personalities and thus enable them to better understand how much of their work reflects themselves and how much depicts objective reality. Although it is not necessary to go to this extreme, the idea has considerable merit; the personality of the investigator can obviously play an important role both in the kinds of material that will be gathered and in what subsequently happens to it. Nowhere is this more true than in the field of life-history research.

Some investigators are much better equipped in terms of personality than others when it comes to working intimately with "exotic" peoples. Similarly, some can deal with deviants such as child abusers, murderers, or the handicapped with less discomfort than others. Some investigators may follow their subjects everywhere, share their food, allow themselves to be fondled and embraced and so on, whereas others may find physical contact repugnant and thus maintain a greater degree of social distance. This naturally affects the kinds of data that can be gathered. Genealogies and certain other kinds of data, for example, can be gathered by strictly formal interviewing in which it is never necessary to lose one's "dignity." There are fieldworkers who work out a regular schedule for interviewing and each day a selected number of informants pass by their desk to be formally interviewed in turn. There is the great danger in this procedure that fact will not be well separated from fantasy and, needless to say, the observations so necessary for reliability are neglected. Other investigators, less inhibited and reserved, may enter into the activity whatever it may be and find no difficulty in crawling into pig houses, delousing both pigs and themselves, eating whatever is given them, and putting up with the most fantastic demands. Some fieldworkers locate their houses right in the village and become more or less integral members of the community, whereas others prefer to build some distance away and maintain more privacy. This matter, of course, is personal; but one should be aware of his or her own limitations and the extent to which they limit the data.

The personality of the investigator also becomes important when attempting to report on native personality. One investigator, for instance, may report that the people are hostile and aggressive where a second, from a different personal background, might perceive them as perfectly "normal" with respect to their aggressivity. The interpretation of behavior is difficult enough because of the cross-cultural variations in meaning that exist, but it can be even more difficult if you have little insight into your own personality. This insight is far more important when attempting a life history than when doing field work in general because, as should be clear, a life history, unlike a biography or an autobiography, is always a delicate and complicated *collaborative* venture. Thus the outcome—the life history itself—is the result of a dual input from two individuals with their own past experiences, biases, interests, needs, and motives.

CHAPTER III

Analysis

The analysis of life histories has always been the least developed aspect of such work. Here we examine some of the most important attempts at analysis by anthropologists and we suggest how methods of analysis that have been employed by members of other disciplines might be applied by anthropologists. Recent life histories are discussed which indicate a trend towards a more self-reflective, phenomenological, and qualitative approach. Again, the collaborative dimension of life-history taking emerges as of increasing concern and importance.

T he earliest life histories by anthropologists included virtually nothing by way of analysis. Sapir's early "The Life of a Nootka Indian" (1921) is a straightforward account of portions of a man's life that focuses primarily on potlatching and in so doing illuminates many features of Nootka culture. Radin's famous *Crashing Thunder* (1926) is similarly unanalyzed, being, as has been previously mentioned, an attempt to portray the life of a typical middle-aged member of the culture. All of the life-history materials that appeared in the 1920s and 1930s were of this essentially nonanalytical type. Most of them appear to have been written to illuminate something about the culture, either the ethos (Wilson 1924, 1928), women's activities (Michelson 1925, 1932, 1933), the "commonplace" or humdrum of the culture (Dyk 1938), the "feel" of the culture (Parsons 1922), or the culture "from within" (Barton 1938). Few, if any, dealt with individuals as such and neither was there any real attempt to "relate the individual to his or her culture."

When Dollard prepared his insightful critique of the life-history method in 1935 he emphasized what he saw as the overwhelming importance of cultures in shaping personality and did not consider the possible effects of individuals or personalities on culture (Allport 1942). This "cultural bias," if you will, is with us yet and, although an interest in individuals as such began to be expressed, the individual *per se* has only occasionally been the primary focus of an anthropological life history. As this is written, there appears to be an increasing interest in the individual.

Simmons, in his 1942 work *Sun Chief*, has an extremely useful chapter on the analysis of life histories. This is not so much an analysis of Don Talayesva's life as it is a series of suggestions about how to go about such analyses. Simmons suggests that individuals be considered as *creature, creator, carrier,* and *manipulator* of the mores of their group, and that some theory of adjustment and/or adaptation is also required for a systematic assessment of the individual's life in relation to the group. Simmons also believed that life histories provided a unique type of data in that they established "a level of continuity in behavior that is more fundamental than either biological, environmental, societal, or cultural determinants, being in fact a synthesis of all four" (1942:396).

David Aberle subsequently did a "psychosocial analysis" of *Sun Chief*, analyzing this single life history, "for the light it sheds on the society in which the subject lives" (1951:1). Aberle attempted to demonstrate how seemingly contradictory accounts of Hopi society could be reconciled by the life-history approach and he also tried to deal with the perennial anthropological problem of relating ideals of behavior with the actual behavior itself. He felt that the life history offered the best means of getting at "the complex relationship of motivations and actions to norms and beliefs" (1951:2). Aberle contended that as the system of beliefs and values that his subject, Don Talayesva, operated with was the same as that of other Hopi, and as the total environment was also the same, "it follows that their interpretations of certain situations will be similar . . . and the consequences will be similar in range" (1951:118). Thus he felt that by looking at Don Talayesva's reactions to the problems he faced we would know something about all Hopi and Hopi society. He argued that this did not imply that Don Talayesva was a typical Hopi nor that the course of his life was typical. He felt that the generalizations that could be made by utilizing his procedure could be made even if Don Talayesva's experiences had been the most extreme of all Hopi and his particular group the most strife-ridden. This proposition is similar to Margaret Mead's claim that "any member of a group, provided that his position within that group is properly specified, is a perfect sample of the group wide pattern on which he is acting as an informant" (1953:648). Although Aberle discusses Don Talayesva's prestige drive, his impotence and anxiety attacks, and other such matters, he does not attempt to explain the causes for such behaviors—there is no formal consideration, that is, of Don Talayesva as a personality (Aberle did not claim to offer any). This remains one of the most ambitious and thoroughgoing attempts at life-history analysis to date but it appears to have stimulated few other such attempts. This is unfortunate, as it would be interesting to know whether the prestige seeking, mistrust, aggression, conformity, and compensatory behaviors that Aberle discusses for the Hopi might not be similar to behaviors in many other cultures and if so, under what conditions they might be either present or absent. There are numerous life-history accounts presently available with sufficient detail to lend themselves to this type of analysis.

A similarly ambitious and detailed "psychobiological personality study" was published two years previous to Aberle's work by the psychiatrists Alexander Leighton and Dorothea Leighton (1949). Here the focus was much more specifically on personality, the personality of the Navaho *Gregorio, The Hand-Trembler*. Even so, Leighton and Leighton attempted the analysis for the light it would ultimately shed on the community: "We believe that a series of such psychobiological personality studies representing samples from various parts of the social group would give a picture of the community that would be informative in proportion to the number, distribution, and completeness of the sample" (1949:1). A further purpose of this study was to illustrate a means for handling and organizing social-science data. Like Aberle, Leighton and Leighton were interested in examining the relationship of the individual to the culture and they attempted to render their data in such a way as to make that goal more easily possible. They were particularly concerned to insure that others could see for themselves the precise data upon which they based their psychodynamic and cultural interpretations.

Being well aware that attempting to deal with the general experiences of an individual's entire life would be out of the question, Leighton and Leighton focused on one central theme of Gregorio's life, his hand-trembling (a form of divination). This, they felt, was less common among the Navaho than farming or sheepherding and thus set Gregorio somewhat apart from most of his contemporaries. Presumably, had further such studies emerged from the Ramah Navaho project, of which Leighton and Leighton were a part, Gregorio's life history would have been only one of what would have been a genuine sample of Navaho; but others were not forthcoming.

The presentation of Gregorio's life by Leighton and Leighton is essentially chronological: childhood, youth, first marriage, hand-trembling, second marriage, and settling down. They present a life chart summarizing the main events and sequences of Gregorio's life and they then turn to a discussion of the equilibrium of Gregorio's life. Gregorio's hand-trembling is examined from the point of view of how it functions as a personal activity contributing to his personal equilibrium and then as a Navaho culture pattern linking Gregorio to his culture. Although by European standards Gregorio's beliefs and behavior as a hand-trembler might be seen as neurotic and delusional, by Navaho standards they clearly are not. As Aberle later did for the Hopi and Sun Chief, Leighton and Leighton tried to demonstrate that most of the important elements in Gregorio's life would be shared by other Navahos. They conclude:

Looking at Gregorio in the light of these findings, it would seem that the major concerns of his life are also the principal concerns of other Navahos in the region. In other words, his preoccupations are not unusual. (1949:38)

The largest portion of *Gregorio, The Hand-Trembler* is taken up with the organization and presentation of fieldnotes. This was done to suggest to others a system of compiling and referencing data and also to make their raw data available to others so they might come to their own conclusions. While this is a desirable procedure, it is virtually impossible at present to publish fieldnotes and there is little indication that others made use of Leighton and Leighton's scheme. Although their discussion of Gregorio as hand-trembler is compelling it could have been carried much further than it was and, as they acknowledged, Gregorio's life could just as easily have been presented around an entirely different theme.

Although there were no further in-depth analyses of individual life histories by anthropologists for a period of almost ten years after the work of Leighton and Leighton and of Aberle, life histories were being gathered and used by anthropologists. This was the period of relatively intense interest in culture-and-personality studies, and life histories were used as the basis for generalizations about "modal personality," "national character," and other such abstract "patterns of culture." Life histories of American blacks were analyzed for recurrent behavior patterns by Davis and Dollard (1940) and similarly by Kardiner and Ovesey (1951). The analysis of multiple life histories was the backbone of DuBois's well-known work, *The People of Alor* (1944), one of the most important of the "basic personality" studies inspired by the collaboration of Kardiner, Linton, DuBois, and West (1945). *The People of Alor* sought to show that there was a "demonstrable relationship between the personalities of adults within a group and the socio-cultural milieu in which they lived" (DuBois 1960:xviii). The life histories were analyzed, along with children's drawings, Porteus Maze Tests, word association tests, and Rorschach protocols, in an attempt to expose this relationship. Although the life histories showed that each of the people had a highly individual character, each also shared features of the Alorese basic personality structure, which was in turn determined by the basic institutions of Alorese culture.

A somewhat similar use of life histories was made by Gladwin and

Sarason in their work on Truk (1953). This study was an outgrowth of DuBois's Alorese work and was intended to develop a useful and quick means to assess personality. Both the Thematic Apperception Test (T.A.T.) and the Rorschach were used, in conjunction with the analysis of dreams and life histories. Gladwin and Sarason were much concerned with sampling and selected 23 individuals who represented both deviant and "average" persons. This research was somewhat unusual in that it featured Sarason's "blind" interpretations of the projective tests, a clinical approach, rather than the more traditional scoring of such tests based upon categories and frequencies. While this analysis was recognized as more subjective, it was believed that it permitted fuller exploitation of the materials produced by the subjects. Using this procedure made it possible for Gladwin and Sarason to examine the ways in which culturally determined perceptual modes affected the response patterns of their subjects, a factor ordinarily observed by interpretations based upon the simple scoring of responses. Here, again, the focus was much more upon culture than upon individual personality.

Morris Carstairs, a psychiatrist with anthropological training, undertook a systematic exploration of high-caste Hindu personality using the life-history approach (1958). Like Gladwin and Sarason, Carstairs was explicitly concerned with sampling. He set out to use 27 informants, all male, nine from each of the three castes he was working with. In each of the three groups he desired to have three eminent persons, three average, and three who were low in the esteem of others. He also attempted to have one older, one middle-aged, and one younger man in each of the groups. Although he did not achieve this distribution in practice, even though he eventually increased his sample size, his work was an advance over previous work.

Carstairs's primary aim in his research was to see if his concepts of personality development were adequate to explain the relationship between adult personality traits and the formation experiences peculiar to the society. He analyzed 37 life histories, using a combination of Adolph Meyer's psychobiological theory and psychoanalytic theory. From these cases he presented generalizations about Hindu interpersonal and family relations, Hindu body-image, religion and fantasy, conscious and unconscious processes. He then presented three of his life histories with commentary so that others could see the applicability and limitations of his interpretive comments. Carstairs himself was acutely aware of the limitations of what he attempted and, although his study remains one of the classics of culture-and-personality research, it was not widely emulated.

As the interest in culture-and-personality studies waned, the formal use of life histories for that purpose began to fall off likewise. And, although anthropologists necessarily depend heavily upon personal accounts, this dependence has not always been consciously appreciated or intensively examined. While anthropological data are in some sense virtually all biographical, we do not always think of them that way.

While the interest in modal personality and national character began to slacken, the interest in life histories themselves actually continued. One of the better ones, which also included some analysis, appeared in 1960. *Worker in the Cane,* by Sidney Mintz, is a rather detailed life history of a Puerto Rican man who, according to Mintz, is in no way "average":

> He is not an "average" anything—neither an average man, nor an average Puerto Rican, nor an average Puerto Rican lower-class sugar cane worker. He has lived just one life and not all of that. He doesn't think of himself as representative of anything, and he is right. His solutions to life's problems may not be the best ones, either, but he seems satisfied with his choices. I have tried to put down his story in the context of what I could understand about the circumstances under which he lived and lives. (1974:ii)

Even though Don Taso is not average, his life does tell us a great deal about the Puerto Rico of his day and especially about the great changes that were taking place. Mintz concentrates on the subject of change but in so doing he also shows how the broader cultural and social changes affect an individual's concept of self and how that process, in turn, affects the motives of individuals, in this case Don Taso. He analyzes Don Taso's seemingly strange religious conversion and is able to demonstrate that it makes sense in the context of the time and in the context of Don Taso's own life. In short, Mintz manages to relate an individual to his culture in a way not usually attempted. He says of this:

> In Taso's case, the crucial events which transformed the barrio affected him in the same way as they did most of his neighbors. But such deeply personal events as his loss of his father while he was still an infant; the early deaths of his mother and sister; the fact that his marriage remained stable in

spite of the suffering he and his wife caused each other; his illness and its cure;
and his entrance into the church—all these are special features of Taso's life,
interwoven with the basic values of his social group and given in each
instance a distinctive quality that is the essence of individual experience and
perception. (1974:263)

Although Mintz's analysis is by no means as detailed and complete as
it might be, it stands as a good example of the potential of the life-history
approach for relating the individual person to change in his or her
culture.

Nancy Oestreich Lurie's *Mountain Wolf Woman* (1961), published at
about the same time as *Worker in the Cane*, contains nothing in the way of
analysis; but Lurie's comments do give some insight into the relationship of Winnebago males and females and into Winnebago attitudes
towards whites. It also tells us something about Mountain Wolf
Woman's famous brother, Crashing Thunder, and the acceptance of the
peyote religion by the Winnebago.

All too often life histories are presented with no more than a few
limited comments rather than some form of systematic analysis.
Winter's *Beyond the Mountains of the Moon* (1965), although a valuable
account of much intrinsic interest, is another case in point. Winter's
brief concluding chapter does say something of value about the position
of women among the Amba, and about certain features of Amba
culture, but it does not represent a true analysis of the life-history
materials.

The same thing is true of the well-known biographical publications
of Oscar Lewis, who has done more than any other anthropologist to
promote the life-history approach. Lewis began his family-biography
approach and developed his notion of a "culture of poverty" with *Five
Families* in 1959. In *Five Families* he recorded in detail a day in the life of
each of the five families. This was followed by the more truly
biographical and very moving *The Children of Sánchez* (1961). In 1964
appeared the life history *Pedro Martinez* and then *La Vida* in 1965. These
works, especially the last three, received much literary acclaim and
achieved a wide popular audience, and rightly so. The concept of a
culture of poverty, although controversial, was widely accepted. These
works did a great deal to popularize anthropology and they represent
probably the best examples of a literary and humanistic anthropology.
Although Lewis occasionally makes assertions about the various

personalities and their motives he makes no attempt at analysis; whatever commentary there is has to do mostly with the culture of poverty. Out of the work of Oscar Lewis also came a three-volume oral history of contemporary Cuba (Lewis, Lewis, and Rigdon 1977a, 1977b, 1978).

Undoubtedly the best example of the presentation of a life history for purely ethnographic purposes is *Apache Odyssey* (1969) by Morris E. Opler. By presenting his subject's account essentially as it was told, with very extensive annotations, Opler gives us an extremely detailed ethnography of Mescalero Apache culture. There is no focus on the subject as an individual personality and no analysis of any kind, although the life history is rich in detail and could have been analyzed from a variety of perspectives.

The first really serious attempt to set forth a scheme for the analysis of life histories since those of Aberle and of Leighton and Leighton was suggested by David G. Mandelbaum in 1973. Using the life of Mahatma Gandhi as an example, Mandelbaum suggests that when analyzing a life history we consider the *dimensions* of a person's life, the principal *turnings*, and the person's characteristic means of *adaptation*.

A dimension, according to Mandelbaum, "is made up of experiences that stem from a similar base and are linked in their effects on the person's subsequent actions." The dimensions actually mentioned by Mandelbaum are the biological, cultural, social, and psychosocial (1973:180). The interplay of biological and cultural dimensions is seen by Mandelbaum as follows:

> The biological factors set the basic conditions for a life course; cultural factors mould the shape and content of a person's career. The *cultural* dimension lies in the mutual expectations, understandings, and behavior patterns held by the people among whom a person grows up and in whose society he becomes a participant. Each culture provides a general scenario for the life course that indicates the main divisions, tells when transitions should be made, and imputes a social meaning to biological events from birth through death. Each scenario interprets and affects the biological dimension in its own way; each provides its own chart for the progress of a life. (1973:180)

Although the cultural and social dimensions of a life overlap, Mandelbaum believes the distinction is analytically useful. The social dimension consists of the social relations the person encounters during his or her life, the roles required of the person, the acts of personal choice characteristic of the group, and the commonly understood ways of working out recurrent conflicts.

By the psychosocial dimension Mandelbaum refers to the individual's feelings, attitudes, and subjective world in general. Although these are individually experienced, each individual's experiences are likely to be similar in important ways to others in the same culture. Mandelbaum also points out, again rightly so, that much more attention has been paid to psychosocial development than to the cultural and social dimensions of life (1973:180).

Turnings, in Mandelbaum's scheme, are the major transitions that a person must make during the course of life. A turning is accomplished "when the person takes on a new set of roles, enters into fresh relations with a new set of people, and acquires a new self-conception" (1973:181). A turning can be either a gradual phenomenon or a single event and it may also be either improvised or in some way prescribed. Even though individuals' own perceptions of their turnings may not be the same as those of an investigator, their perceptions will, in fact, influence their lives.

Adaptations "are changes that have a major effect on a person's life and on his basic relations with others" (1973:181). They are behaviors that contribute to survival. Adaptation, according to Mandelbaum,

> . . . is a built-in process, because every person must, in the course of his life, alter some of his established patterns of behavior to cope with new conditions. Each person *changes* his ways in order to maintain *continuity*, whether of group participation or social expectation or self-image or simply survival. Some of these new conditions are imposed by his own physical development. Others arise from changing external conditions, whether of custom or climate, family or society. (1973:181)

Using his conceptual framework, Mandelbaum analyzed the life of Gandhi and illustrated clearly that such a framework did indeed help in organizing and understanding an individual's life. Although there were some skeptics among those who reviewed and commented on his paper, generally it met with a positive response and it remains as probably the most important scheme available for gathering and interpreting the lives of others. Furthermore, unlike earlier approaches, this one has actively stimulated others to attempt similar analyses.

James M. Freeman (1979), for example, has written an extremely fascinating and detailed life history of an Indian untouchable which, although it employs Mandelbaum's scheme to good effect, offers a disappointingly brief chapter devoted to analysis. His materials are so rich, however, that either Freeman himself or someone else could easily expand on or reanalyze them. Freeman does present a very useful discussion of his own role in the taking and presentation of Muli's life history and makes it clear just how collaborative an experience it is.

When Melford Spiro reviewed culture-and-personality research in 1972 and called for a reorientation, he argued that whereas personality in such studies had always been seen as *explanandum* it should be changed to become *explanans* (1972:585). For life-history studies this distinction means that rather than concentrating on how the particular individual was shaped by the culture we should concentrate on how the individual shapes or perpetuates the culture. How, that is, do the motives, beliefs, and acts of individuals interact with the environment and with significant others to create and maintain that abstraction we conceive of as culture? This question, he pointed out, was the sadly neglected dimension of a field that had concentrated heavily on the effect of culture upon personality and upon personality as an intervening variable. One of the few people who have actually attempted to deal with this is Charles C. Hughes who, in his life history *Eskimo Boyhood: An Autobiography in Psychosocial Perspective* (1974), following Spiro's lead, used the analysis of roles to this end:

> . . . how do human societies get their members to behave in conformity with cultural norms? Or, alternatively, how do they induce their members to perform culturally prescribed roles?
>
> It is at this juncture in the analysis that the concept of personality becomes salient for the understanding of human social systems, for it is in the concept of role that personality and social systems intersect. If personality is viewed as an organized system of motivational tendencies, then it may be said to consist, among other things, of needs and drives. Since modes of drive-reduction and need-satisfaction in man must be learned, one of the functions of personality is the promotion of physical survival, interpersonal adjustment, and intrapersonal integration by organizing behavior for the reduction of its drives and the satisfaction of its needs. If some of these needs can then be satisfied by means of culturally prescribed behavior—if, that is, social roles are capable of satisfying personality needs—these needs may serve to motivate the performance of the roles. But if social systems can function only if their constituent roles are performed, then, in motivating the

performance of roles, personality not only serves its own functions but it becomes a crucial variable in the functioning of social systems as well. (Spiro 1961:100)

Hughes analyzes the roles of apprentice hunter, schoolboy, and son (to father) as they are played out by his subject, Nathan Kakianak. He selected these specific roles because "they represent aspects of the sociocultural environment which structure major areas of the life space, not only for the subject of this life history but for many others in the community as well" (Hughes 1974:386).

Although Hughes' attempt to show how it is that when personality motivates the performance of roles it at the same time meets the needs of the social system is not as convincing as it might be (Langness 1975), it remains a pioneering, worthwhile, and virtually unique attempt to deal concretely with the complex issue of relating personality to social system. In fact, it is one of the few serious attempts by an anthropologist to employ role analysis at all and for that reason alone is worthy of attention. Hughes also employs role analysis in an attempt to understand the process of socialization:

If, then, "socialization" is a process that necessarily occurs over time and in a context of public social events, we can turn to a life history and use the concrete details presented in it for illustrating some of the dimensions of that process. Through the eyes of a person who lived them, can we not see the many ways in which "culture" or "society" interacts with an evolving human being, presenting daily dilemmas not only of conflict, decision, and threat but also of pleasure, achievement, and success? With behavioral detail, can we not close that synapse between "person" and "group" and in so doing convey a sense of the creative dimensions of what we call "socialization"? (1974:384)

Here we think Hughes is more successful. Through his careful examination of Nathan's roles we do understand better the boy emerging as a man and as a functioning member of his society strongly motivated to be successful in all of the roles he is called upon to perform. "Life histories are notoriously difficult to analyze," Hughes observes (1974:388). He then offers his limited role analysis as a way around this difficulty. It is an attempt well worth emulating.

There is probably no better example of how an individual actually shapes and changes culture patterns than John G. Kennedy's account of the Nubian, Shatr Muhammad Shalashil. Shalashil's account of how he secretly and single-handedly worked to change the brutal defloration customs associated with traditional Nubian weddings indicates how difficult and slow change is even under the influence of an innovative and respected leader. As his own experience was so distasteful to him he embarked upon a campaign to spare others the experience:

> After I came to settle in Kanuba, I made a secret campaign against the practice of having a *mashta* [a slave woman present] on the wedding night. I avoided discussing this with the old men, who like to keep the Nubian tradition, and only made my remarks to young men, especially those who were about to marry. Of course, young men are eager to have intercourse the first night, so I knew they would be receptive to my ideas. I vividly described my unfortunate experiences, urged them to eliminate the *mashta* and to use the penis instead of their fingers. I also urged them to insist on meeting the bride before their marriage. I said, "How can a man have intercourse with a woman to whom he has not spoken even one word? Islam is against that." (Kennedy 1977:114)

Shalashil was successful in his attempts if only in influencing a number of his relatives and friends, but of course that is how all such changes begin. He brought about changes in other areas of his culture as well.

Kennedy also confronted the question of the degree to which a life history can stand alone. He attempted to blend a cultural and historical context with a life history in order to overcome the foreignness of the Nubian situation for a primarily English-speaking public. This device does make Shalashil's innovations and motives much easier to understand. It is a more skillful mixture of ethnography and biography than is ordinarily found and, as in the case of Hughes, is the kind of attempt that should be carried further by others. The question raised here is more important than one might think as it involves the fundamental issue of cross-cultural communication. Consider, for example, the question of what William H. Gass calls "nonfictitious nature":

> Nonfictitious nature has its way about a good deal. If in a story it rains, the streets usually get wet; if a man is stabbed, he bleeds; smoke can still be a sign of fire, and screams can be sounds of damsels in distress. No novel is without its assumptions. It is important to find them out, for they are not always the

same assumptions the reader is ready, unconsciously, to make. Hawthorne could count on more than Henry James, as James complained. Do we any longer dare to infer goodness from piety, for example, evil from promiscuity, culture from rank? (1970:23)

It is not only novels, of course, that involve assumptions, and clearly the assumptions involved when writing within a culture are not the same as those asociated with writing cross-culturally. Assuming that rain will make things wet may be fair enough, but to infer evil from promiscuity would be obvious nonsense, goodness from piety the same. And what about the concept of "damsels in distress"? Although Kennedy does not pursue the issue of cross-cultural communication as such it is clear that the question of how much sharing of emotion, understanding, or even "humanness" in general can be assumed is much on his mind. The context he provides is basically an attempt to eliminate unwarranted assumptions.

In a brilliantly provocative recent work, *Tuhami: Portrait of a Moroccan* (1980), Vincent Crapanzano attempts to deal directly with the nature of the assumptions involved in doing life history and ethnographic research. By including himself in the analysis, and reflecting carefully upon his own beliefs and values, Crapanzano is able to provide us with a more useful understanding of the process of life-history work than has previously been available. He demonstrates rather convincingly that by leaving themselves out of their accounts previous ethnographers have given a false picture of ethnography and what it can reveal. He says:

> The ethnographer's entry into the field is always a separation from his world of primary reference—the world through which he obtains, and maintains, his sense of self and his sense of reality. He is suddenly confronted with the possibility of Otherness, and his immediate response to this Otherness is to seek both the security of the similar and the distance and objectivity of the dissimilar. No longer bound to the conventions of similarity and dissimilarity that obtain within his own world of reference, he vacillates between an overemphasis on the similar or on the dissimilar; at times, especially under stress, he freezes his relationship with—his understanding of—this Otherness. He may become overly rigid, and his rigidity may determine the "texts" he elicits and the form he gives them. He may, in his anxiety, attempt to arrest time. Fortunately, the field experience is a lived experience that perdures, permitting a certain learning and requiring a flexibility that militates against this tendency to freeze both the relation with, and the understanding of, Otherness. Fortunately, too, most ethnographic

encounters are, despite even the ethnographer, very human experiences. The savage is, so to speak, less cowed by the ethnographer than the ethnographer is by the savage. (1980:137–138)

Tuhami is an important and challenging experiment that demands serious consideration by all ethnographic fieldworkers and one that bears repeating by those whose primary interest is in the study of lives.

Peter Wilson's fascinating and unusual account of Oscar Bryan is an attempt to "describe the relationship of a society to its members" (1975:x). Oscar is a "madman" on the tiny island of Providencia in the Caribbean. He exists in a complex and tenuous relationship with the other members of his society, being tolerated, and in a strange way even respected, but at the same time feared. Wilson's analysis of this kind of "love-hate" relationship not only tells us something about Oscar as an individual, but also a great deal about how an individual manipulates and controls the social system in which he or she is immersed. It also makes some interesting comments on the relationship of "madness" to authority, to privacy, to power, to reciprocity, and, finally, to the trust that is required to maintain social relations at all. Unlike Hughes and Crapanzano, who draw eclectically from psychological theory, Wilson employs no explicit psychological theory at all. Nonetheless, through his use of Oscar's life history, he says something of importance about the nature of insanity. As both Tuhami and Oscar are recognized by their respective societies as deviants, an interesting comparison might be drawn between the two cases. Further, as one author is self-reflexive in his writing and the other not, an interesting comparison of ethnographic styles is also suggested.

Another study that eschews explicit psychological theory and focuses primarily upon the relationship of individuals to their social system is Jane Holden Kelley's *Yaqui Women* (1978). Often the analysis of a life history is virtually inseparable from the description itself. This work is an example and it is interesting to note what Kelley has said about it:

The basic tenet underlying this exercise in collecting life histories is that individualized data can contribute an important dimension for anthropological problems that may respond more sensitively to analysis on this scale of magnitude. The broad concern guiding the research from the beginning was an interest in factors affecting the structuring of interpersonal relationships and adaptive strategies in the face of alternatives. More specific topics for interpretation were generated in the course of field work and at later stages. In other words, the methodology was broadly inductive after the initial orientation, with an ongoing interplay between raw data and interpretive framework. Consideration of the structuring of interpersonal relationships and adaptive strategies exercised by each woman forms the connective tissue for the interpretive treatment of each woman's story. (1978:31)

In fact, as Norman B. Schwartz has recently pointed out, a biography as such is itself an analytic scheme:

In one sense, a biography as such is an analytic scheme. When [Kirkpatrick] writes that *all* biography "attempts to describe adult behavior and to relate it to antecedent experiences which dispose the subject to deal with the world in characteristic ways," and then adds that this adult behavior results from the encounter between character and circumstance, she is making several analytic assumptions. To take an obvious example, we could as readily assume that behavior shapes character rather than vice versa, hence her perspective is as analytic as any other. (1977:94)

That a biography is an analytic scheme is undoubtedly related to the fact that so many published life histories appear to have had no formal analysis—the analytic scheme and assumptions are simply built into the biographical materials themselves. This is an area that has not been given enough attention.

Another method for looking at selected aspects of lives, used by Edgerton and Langness (1978) in their research on the mentally retarded, is a form of event analysis similar to the critical-incident technique (Flanagan 1954; Fivars 1973). By concentrating on incidents that either facilitate or hinder a "normal" life style for the mildly retarded, Edgerton and Langness are able to better uncover and understand the process involved in an individual's adjustment and adaptation to his or her cultural milieu. This method for the study of a normalization incident involves three standard features: (1) multiple points of view, (2) a longitudinal perspective, and (3) ecological context. In brief, *multiple points of view* refers to the procedure of eliciting the accounts of all persons whose views are relevant to the incident; *longitudinal perspective* is added by the fact that with years of prior work there is a background of recorded observations that bear upon the incident; *ecological context* means that by pursuing each incident to its saturation point all relevant environmental factors can be assessed. Although Edgerton and Langness employ this approach specifically to understand the normalization process (Wolfensberger 1972), there is no reason why it could not be employed more widely in the study of lives. In fact, in a way it is, as Barbara Myerhoff, in her 1978 study of the aged, employs a very similar type of approach, one she developed out of Victor Turner's earlier work on social drama (1957).

Often the conceptual scheme that informs a life history is taken from the subject's culture itself. An individual's life history is used to illustrate the normal progression of an individual through the various stages of life prescribed by the society in which he or she lives, the stages being determined by the investigator's prior knowledge of the culture. George Grinnell's early work, *When Buffalo Ran* (1920), for example, is a kind of fictionalized life history of a Plains Indian's life, passing through a number of culturally prescribed steps, and then culminating with the coming of Europeans and the passing of the buffalo. *Juan the Chamula* (Pozas 1962) is a very similar type of account, as are *Jim Whitewolf: The Life of a Kiowa Apache Indian* (Brant 1969), and many many others.

That life histories would have sometimes taken this form is not surprising given that, as Mandelbaum made clear, anthropologists have employed only two main approaches to the study of lives:

> In their observation of the development of a person, anthropologists have used two main approaches: life passage studies and life history studies. Life passage (or life cycle) studies emphasize the requirements of society, showing how the people of a group socialize and enculturate their young in order to make them into viable members of society. Life history studies, in contrast, emphasize the experiences and requirements of the individual—how the person copes with society rather than how society copes with the stream of individuals. This difference in emphasis in anthropological studies is also found in sociological and psychological studies. (1973:177)

Mandelbaum did not comment on the fact that life histories have so often been presented as representative of the typical life cycle, nor, although he was well aware of the possibility, did he consider in any detail the fact that the culturally prescribed stages, part of what he termed "dimensions," would themselves influence the "turnings" and "adaptations" in important ways. Alexander Moore, in an interesting comparison of Indian and Ladino life cycles published in the same year as Mandelbaum's article (1973), makes it clear that the culturally defined life-cycle stages of the Indian community help to produce an individual very different from those that one finds in the less structured and more individualized system of the Ladino community. As Schwartz summed it: "If an Indian biography may be described in terms of group-centered, ascribed turnings, a Ladino biography may be described in terms of ego-centered, self-chosen or at least self-manipulated turnings" (1977:97). Schwartz's analysis of his life-history subject, Abel, building on the work of Mandelbaum and Moore, demonstrates perhaps as well as anyone has done that biographies are cultural as well as idiosyncratic documents, and that even the concept of "self," as Hallowell pointed out (1955), is itself culturally conditioned. Recent life-history work, informed by the insights of Mandelbaum, Wilson, Hughes, Schwartz, and others, and increasingly stimulated also by more phenomenologically oriented researchers (see, for example, Crapanzano 1977b, 1980; Watson 1976; Frank 1979a), promises to dramatically improve both the quantity and quality of life-history research in the future.

In spite of these recent and very promising developments in anthropology, it remains that anthropologists in general have given less attention to formal schemes for the analysis of life histories and life cycles, and to methodological issues as well, than have members of other disciplines. And in spite of their professed willingness to borrow from others, methodologically and analytically, anthropologists have only rarely attempted to apply the schemes of others to their own life-history materials. There are many such schemes available.

Leonard Cain has reviewed much of the work that has been done relating life course to social structure (1964). Although it has been well known at least since Van Gennep's pioneering work (1960) that all societies recognize change in status as one passes through the life course, and that they most often mark these changes with various rites of passage, the implications of this status change for social structure have not been as carefully explored as they should. Thus it would be possible to examine individual lives as they either deviate from or approach the cultural norm (or ideal) for the life course and then consider how this event pattern affects such things as demography, family structure, and the wider network of kin. While it is well known, for example, that rites of passage result in formal or informal age grades that often are an important feature of social structure, the actual process involved can be understood only through an examination of the cumulating effect of individual lives as they contribute to the process.

Cain has also called attention to the relative lack of studies of adult socialization, another area where life histories would be of great utility. Even though there is good reason to believe that adult socialization is of great importance in anticipating age statuses, and perhaps is as important as childhood socialization for personality formation, such studies still lag far behind studies of childrearing (Brim and Wheeler 1966). Levinson, working with a number of others (Levinson et al. 1974) and using a life-history approach, has focused on developmental periods in the adult life course with special emphasis on the "mid-life transition." Similar attempts, particularly cross-culturally conducted, would be an invaluable contribution to our knowledge of this experience.

Similarly, although the concept of "career" has been systematicallly explored by social scientists and others from at least the 1930s (Bühler 1935; Hughes 1937) to the present, the use of life histories for this purpose has not been extensive. Intensive life histories would seem to be demanded if, following Hughes and Cain, you distinguish between objective and subjective perspectives on career:

> Objectively, career, in a rigidly structured system, is a "series of statuses and clearly defined offices." Even if the division of labor is not highly structured, jobs typically include "sequences of position, achievement, responsibility, and even of adventure." Subjectively, in contrast, career is the "moving perspective in which the person sees his life as a whole and inter- prets the meaning of his various attributes, actions, and the things which happen to him." (Hughes 1937:409–410).

As Becker and Strauss have pointed out, "A frame of reference for studying careers is, at the same time, a frame for studying personal identities" (1956). Questions of personal identity, how identity is linked to career, age statuses, or whatever, have scarcely been undertaken on a cross-cultural basis. Peter Wilson's remarkable work *Oscar: An Inquiry into the Nature of Sanity* (1975) is a rare and valuable exception.

Likewise, if one is interested in the phenomenon of "age-status asynchronization," that is, in those age-status discontinuities that occur in many people's lives, individual life histories are the only means of proceeding. The experience of becoming a college student at 65, being tried for murder as an adult at 15, or being married to a person 30 years your junior or senior, for example, cannot be meaningfully examined in the abstract. Similarly, it would be most rewarding to know if mentally retarded persons pass through the same presumed "stages of life" that others do and if not, why not. Studying the lives of such persons would be an obvious and important approach to the concept of age-status asynchronization.

Studies of deviance would seem to ideally require life histories. To move beyond statistical frequencies and superficial explanations it is crucial to understand not only the biological, cultural, and social influences but also the individual factors that come together to produce acts of deviance. Perspectives on mental illness, criminality, mental retardation, and other forms of deviance can be enormously expanded through the examination of particular cases (Bogdan 1974; Bogdan and Taylor 1976; Koegel 1978; Shaw 1930; Whittemore, Koegel, and Langness 1980). Again, particular cases from a variety of cultures would be most useful in this regard (Edgerton 1976).

. There have been many attempts to determine if there is some kind of "ground plan," "life course," "life-history structure," "passages," or "anatomy" for people's lives and, if so, whether people share the same plan (Dailey 1971). Else Frenkel, in discussing the work of Charlotte Bühler (1933), who over a number of years undertook a large-scale study of four hundred biographies in order to determine if there was some kind of life plan, concludes that there is. Bühler and Frenkel argue that there are "rather sharply demarcated *phases* through which every person passes in the course of his life" (Frenkel 1936:2), and that each of these phases is characterized by a set of concrete traits which are shared in common at each phase. The aim of this investigation was to describe "the psychological development of human beings, and to attempt to determine the regularity with which the various periods of life succeed one another in this development" (Frenkel 1936:3). Bühler and Frenkel thought it would be possible to develop a notion of *psychological age*, as some people appeared to pass through the phases either earlier or later than the average. From this they believed they might even derive a *psychological quotient* for the personal-development status of the individual. Had this notion been established it could have been used, they thought, to determine whether an individual's "psychological profile" corresponds to his or her age. This correspondence would presumably have been useful to physicians and to employers of all kinds as well.

Bühler (Bühler and Massarik 1968) eventually posited five periods in a person's life:

1. Progressive growth without reproductive ability (roughly 0–15 years).
2. Progressive growth with the onset of reproductive ability (roughly 15–25 years.)
3. Reproductive ability and stationary growth (25 to 45 or 50).
4. Beginning decline and loss of reproductive ability in the female (45 or 50 to 65 or 70).
5. Further decline and loss of reproductive ability in one or both sexes (65 to 70 and beyond). (Sundberg 1977)

These periods are related by Bühler to the development of life goals, the reassessment of those goals, and to the roles assigned by the society on the basis of age. Naturally, not all people fit precisely into this scheme, but inasmuch as it is linked to physical vitality and maturation some types of activity reach their peak at an earlier age than others. Mental activity can reach great heights later in life whereas physical activity tends to peak earlier. This general outline of a life has been widely accepted and elaborated upon by others.

Erik Erikson (1968) has suggested eight stages of life which correspond to the chronology by which individuals acquire new capacities and deal with the problems that arise at each stage. The problems or conflicts that arise, Erikson believes, stem from both the biological maturation of the organism and the sociocultural setting it experiences. Others, including Jung, have also talked of various stages or patterns that characterize human lives, such as the "morning" or "afternoon" of life. Dailey has summed up the situation with respect to stages as follows:

There are, in brief, richly promising suggestions from the different theories as to what these grand divisions of life are, along with a lack of suggestions as to how one can empirically find them in data.

Time is the substance one is dividing here, but there are many times to divide. One may speak of chronologic, sociological (age, career, timetables that accompany certain games and roles), and emotional timetables unique to the individual (for example, anniversary depressions). There are psychological orientations to time: the past, present, and future perspectives, as in Lewin's model. There are cycles to consider, from diurnal cycles to annual calendars; some such cycles are clearly biochemical in origin and some require an appreciation of the ethnic and cultural timetables (1971:43).

Dailey goes on to suggest that life-history assessment must assume, as above, some kind of macrostructure or basic anatomy for a life and then go on to progressively smaller units of analysis. He speaks of "recurring thema" or "plots," "particular thema," "learning sequences," and—what he regards as the smallest unit for meaningful analysis—the "episode." The further assumption is that there are interconnections among the episodes and thus that the life history is intelligible as a whole.

Certainly the idea of stages has been a useful heuristic, but whether or not there are truly useful universal life stages remains an open question and one to which anthropologists, with their broader cross-cultural view, could make a contribution. "Ethnic and cultural time-tables" remain to be systematically examined.

Yet another way to order life histories is through the idea of "life crises." Riegel has recently suggested that "crises, conflicts, and contradictions ought to be regarded as constructive confrontations and as the basis for development rather than in a negative manner and as causes for disruption" (1974:99). He goes on to argue that there is a dialectic to development which results in the continuous growth and change of the individual as he or she confronts life crises. Far from deeming this confrontation pathological, he regards it as the essentially normal course of adult life and goes on to examine the lives of Piaget and Wundt in contrast to the lives of more ordinary adults.

Similarly, Holmes and Rahe (1967) developed a means for scoring life stresses that result from the kinds of changes individuals necessarily undergo—deaths in the family, marriage, illnesses, changes of location, surgery, and so on. If an individual scores high on this scale, presumably he or she is much more likely to become ill than someone who has experienced less stress. Those who have employed this technique claim that it predicts for Japanese as well as for Americans (Holmes and Masuda 1973). As far as we know, no anthropologist (and few if any others) has ever attempted an intensive life history using an individual's stress points as the underlying structure. It would be interesting to compare the kinds, occasions, and amounts of stress people undergo in different cultures, and how they subjectively experience it, a procedure that should, of course, involve the use of intensive life histories. One of the real shortcomings of the Holmes and

Rahe procedure is that it employs a basic questionnaire and leaves the greater number of the potentially most important issues untouched. Certainly there are individual differences in reactions to stress and many people who should be in dire straits indeed, according to the Holmes questionnaire, simply do not react in a predictable manner.

Recent years have seen a growth of interest in psychobiography. This has been defined as "any life history which employs an explicit personality theory" (Glad 1973:296). Virtually all who have actually attempted psychobiographies have employed some variety of depth psychology, that is, some notion of personality that acknowledges unconscious motivations. Probably the best known of such works are Erikson's works on Martin Luther (1958) and Gandhi (1969).

Psychobiographies have become more and more popular in political science although there are many critics of such attempts. Analyses have been attempted of Khrushchev (Wedge 1968) and Nixon (Mazlish 1972), for example, as well as of lesser public officials such as Charles Evans Hughes (Glad 1966), Senators Borah and Fulbright (Glad 1969), and various revolutionaries (Wolfenstein 1967) as well. Most often these attempt to understand such things as charisma, role performance, recruitment to office, political attitudes, and so forth. Although there have been some excesses, there is much to be said for the use of a specific personality theory in the examination of a life history. For an excellent discussion of the use of psychobiography by political scientists, and a cautionary conclusion that deserves attention by all who work with life histories, see Betty Glad:

> Though the psychobiographer cannot eliminate elements of subjectivity in his work, certain restraints and principles of validation should govern his approach. Depth psychology, for example, may direct him to details, many of them quite elusive, which are ignored in traditional studies; nevertheless, he must be guided by the usual tests for documentation followed in history and the social sciences. The sources of his data must be given, so that his facts are susceptible to an outside check; and his explanatory framework should be explicitly presented, so that it may be judged by other scholars in terms of its ability to handle the data in an economic and internally consistent way that accords with the broad body of social science theory and data. (1973:321)

One of the most consistent arguments for the use of life histories has been the holistic nature of the approach—that is, seeing the individual personality as a whole, functioning within the larger sociocultural context of his or her life. The alternative to a holistic approach is to take bits and pieces of a person's life removed from context and examined merely piecemeal. In truth, you can never understand an individual "wholly," but nonetheless there is merit in the attempt. An intensive life history does permit one to understand aspects of both behavior and action that would not otherwise make sense.

There are doubtless ways to structure and analyze life histories other than those we have mentioned briefly here. What is most important to remember in life-history analysis, whatever means you are attempting, is that you are imposing form on that which, although not totally without form, takes on form only in the process of its construction. While there may be very general stages in the course of an ordinary life, individual persons recognize or ignore such stages and/or pass through them early or late. And their own interpretations of their life events may not correspond to those of investigators. Subjective meanings cannot be completely shared and one person's experiences color his or her interpretations of another's. We repeat, constructing a life history is a collaborative act. It is of the utmost importance to be aware of this collaboration and to carefully consider the categories, forms, stages, hypotheses, and theories that emerge in the life-history process. Self-consciousness is as vital as consciousness of the other. Only insofar as you can understand all of the steps in your analysis, and communicate them to others, can you be said to have completed a useful or meaningful life history.

CHAPTER **IV**

Biography and the Structure of Lives

In this chapter, the terms "autobiography," "biography," and "life history" are defined and these forms are compared for what they can reveal about the subject's life. Also examined are the different ways that a "self," a "person," and an individual "life" are looked at in various cultures and contexts. The authors suggest that the meaning of lives can be understood best by also considering the meaning of death in a particular culture.

A life history is a text. If a text is a selection of elements from a life, what is the underlying reality that is being represented? Is a life simply the accumulation of all the events that happened between an individual's birth and death? Does it include only those experiences of which the individual was conscious, only those which are recalled and therefore meaningful? Is there anything comparable between one life and another, particularly if the lives are those of individuals who live in vastly different cultures? Is there anything universal about life itself?

Our answer is perhaps more than scientific. We agree with philosopher Abraham Heschel (1965) that each life harbors a mystery. Our motives are hidden, even from ourselves. Our dreams and our impulses surprise us. And with every action we are capable of surpassing what we already are. Our future is unpredictable, the past indefinite. There is no way to map the boundaries of the soul and no system for calculating its contents. As social scientists, our understanding of lives is always constrained by the models and concepts we employ. We need to keep in mind that any view we may take is partial; no perspective includes all perspectives. Our attempts to define a life fall short and should fall short. Were we able to make some final judgment about what a life is, we would soon, if true to science as we know it, attempt to make our lives fit that definition. This would be a loss. Any one concept about life is never as rich as the reality it points to.

But this partial view is not all, because the symbols and images that people use in telling about their experiences do give substance and texture to the very lives they lead. As we will see later in this chapter, when discussing the life history of a retarded man who found out that his intelligence really is normal, a person's entire sense of self can be transformed because some symbolic element of his or her identity has been changed. For this reason, the life history plays a very special role in our understanding of people's lives, by giving us a method of eliciting the images through which in fact people do see themselves. The question of how these images are received by the life historian during the process of research is critical and complex.

Equally critical and complex is what the reader does with the life history text once it is completed and published. When reading an autobiography, a biography, or a life history, we hear the voice of someone putting us in touch with the experiences, thoughts, and feelings of another's life. The words take shape as images in our minds, as in the unfolding of a drama or the sudden moments of illumination in a poem. Through this process we arrive at a general understanding of the person whose story we are reading or hearing. Step by step, we distill that person's essence, weaving our characterizations around themes provided by the text. Sometimes these themes are made explicit by the author; sometimes it seems that we come up with these themes ourselves. Because we usually can turn only to the text with our questions, and rarely to the speaker personally, our understanding of the actual life depends on the correspondence between the story and the life itself and upon our relationship as readers to the images evoked. What, for instance, is included in the story? How is it interpreted? Who tells it? What must we know in advance in order to understand the things we are told? How much is left to our imagination, and how accurate are the links that our imagination provides? These questions and others are explored in the sections that follow. (See also Frank 1979a.) The answers are as elusive as the questions themselves are fascinating, and anyone who engages in life-history work finds that they crop up again and again. We will start, then, by considering what the basic differences are between an autobiography and a biography for understanding an individual person's life.

Autobiography: The Unaccompanied Voice

To put it simply, autobiographies are reports by individuals about their own lives; what distinguishes them from biography is that the author and subject are one and the same person. The authors of autobiographies typically narrate those events that went into making them unique persons. Exceptional experiences, or at least the precise constellation of events that compose this particular life, are detailed—usually in the order in which they happened. And, presumably, these are events that strongly affected the author's sense of self because, as one critic suggests, the author of an autobiography would have no reason to write one unless some sort of inner transformation had occurred. If the writer were not talking about inner changes, the account would properly belong to history rather than autobiography, since all the events related would be external (Starobinski 1971).

Generally speaking, the intent of anthropologists who have taken life histories of people in non-Western societies has been to record authentic autobiographies, just as they might have been written if the subject were literate. But if an autobiography is, by definition, an account that focuses on the inner life, a very interesting problem arises, because there is evidence that not all people conceive of an "inner self," nor do they have the same ideas as those prevalent in contemporary Western cultures about personal development or change. Can we assume, then, that autobiographies collected by anthropologists in other cultures really reflect the subject's authentic perspective? This is a question that, surprisingly perhaps, anthropologists have not been asking for very long. Yet it is important when using personal documents, such as the "autobiographies" collected cross-culturally, to consider what the individual's concept of the "self," as constituted by his or her culture, may be.

Looking at this question in relation to the role of the individual person in law and ritual in several societies, simple and complex, present and past, Marcel Mauss (1938) proposes that all individuals who have ever lived have had a sense of themselves as unified beings. Taking this further, A.I. Hallowell (1955) suggests a framework for comparing the self cross-culturally by looking at what he called the "behavioral environment." By this, he means to examine how reality becomes structured for individuals from the moment of birth on, as they are socialized to accept certain experiences as related to the self. Among the orientations within the behavioral environment that could be examined cross-culturally, one is especially relevant to the life-history method. This is the "spatiotemporal" orientation. In our own culture this presumes, for example, that an individual can be in only one place at a time or that a person only lives once. These are presumptions not necessarily shared by members of other cultures. But the expectation that all cultures do provide such orientations (whatever their specific contents) is justified by Hallowell on the *a priori* grounds that social relations depend on individuals maintaining a continuous identity through which they take responsibility for proper behavior. If individuals could float freely in society without an established identity to which their actions are attributed, the moral life on which the survival of the group depends would be impossible.

It is interesting to realize that even in the West the concept of the self has undergone tremendous metamorphosis, according to the available evidence. In a two-volume work that is as absorbing as it is scholarly,

Georg Misch (1973) examines this problem. Beginning with Egyptian tomb inscriptions and the monuments on which Mesopotamian despots proclaimed their deeds, Misch charts the expression of self-consciousness in antiquity from the simplest of narrative formulas to the full-blown personal accounts that became prevalent by the fifth century A.D. In Misch's view, autobiography has a philosophical pre-eminence over biography as a record of an individual's self-awareness. He offers two reasons for this assertion: First, autobiographers have all the facts at their disposal, while biographers always work through sources other than this kind of primary introspection. Second, auto-biographers know the significance of the facts in relation to the whole at any time. These are powerful arguments in favor of turning to autobiographies rather than biographies whenever the question is one of understanding the subject's own point of view. This is not to imply, however, that an autobiography is always more accurate than a biography or that persons' interpretations of themselves are necessarily those most justified. As was pointed out by Gordon Allport (1942:125–142), in his still essential guide to the use of personal documents in psychology, autobiographers may fail to mention certain things delib-erately or unintentionally and may be blind to their own motives. Despite these qualifications, Misch's assertion is clearly correct. If, as Misch suggests, the history of autobiography is also the history of self-awareness (at least in the West), then the ability to introspect has expanded along with the literary form. As an historical psychologist has put this point aptly, James Joyce took up as much space in *Ulysses* to describe the internal adventures of half a day as Rousseau required in his *Confessions*, written 150 years earlier, to relate the story of half his life; nourished by the enthusiasm of twentieth-century psychology, he concludes, the inner self has grown to be a complicated affair (Van den Berg 1964).

Autobiography as Self-Transformation

The term "autobiography" is of fairly recent coinage, as words go. The Oxford English Dictionary dates its appearance at 1809. Before that time, and for some time after, there were only two forms of literary self-disclosure: the confession and the memoir. Letters and diaries were not yet seen as genres in this sense, the way they are viewed today, although much energy was devoted to them. The confession, writes James Cox (1971), was an account of an individual's private life, centering on emotions, feelings, secrets, and frustrations, while the memoir was more like a chronicle of events in the person's career. Both forms have been used extensively throughout Western history. Notably there is Augustine's *Confessions* (1961; written 397), which recounts a fourth-century pagan's conversion to Christianity, and the *Confessions* of Jean-Jacques Rousseau (1954), the eighteenth-century philosopher who describes the process of his disengagement from the conventional morality of his times.

As Cox sees it, autobiography has a special place in American culture. He calls to mind that the new nation's first book was Benjamin Franklin's *Memoirs* (1949), written at the same time as Rousseau's *Confessions*. The contemporaneity of these works is suggestive, since in Cox's view the American and French Revolutions released the individual as a potent political entity and gave us the prototype of the modern person. It should be noted that many of America's literary classics are autobiographical. Among these, one would have to include Henry David Thoreau's collection of essays from his journal, published as *Walden* (1893); the poems written in the first-person singular by Walt Whitman (1855); Booker T. Washington's account of his liberation from slave to educator and leader of black Americans, *Up from Slavery* (1963); Gertrude Stein's portrait of her life among the expatriate artists of Paris in the 1920s, *The Autobiography of Alice B. Toklas* (1933), and, perhaps even more significant because their experimental style conveys a new awareness of the way the modern mind operates, Stein's *The Making of Americans* (1934) and *Everybody's Autobiography* (1937). Another landmark work is *The Education of Henry Adams* (1918), in which the scion of one of America's first families confronts the changes in the modern world that have rendered his background and training irrelevant. Also to be considered among these classic statements of personal experience are the lucid yet moving early essays of James Baldwin, *Notes of a Native Son* (1955), many of which were written while residing abroad; and the narrative of a man whose consciousness was raised from street-wise self-interest to an internationalist's perception of the world-wide struggle of black people against racist oppression, *The Autobiography of Malcolm X* (1966), written with the assistance of Alex Haley, who later wrote *Roots* (1976), his own family history and a classic.

This list must be inadequate because the sources that deserve to be mentioned are many, especially if we were also to include works in which an autobiographical element is submerged within a fictional style. Allport (1942), for one, advised life-history researchers to look at creative writings and other artistic products as valid sources for the study of personality, along with the more conventional personal documents that they collect. More recently, one life historian has raised the argument that authors often reveal more about themselves in fiction than in a straightforward autobiographical account (Mintz 1979). He quotes a well-known novelist who writes that in a sense one knows more about Balzac and Dickens from their novels than about Rousseau and Casanova from their Confessions. The reasoning behind such an assertion, in part, is that writers of fiction can tell about things that propriety demands be withheld in a biography or memoir. To turn again just to the more obvious works of autobiography we have mentioned, a striking feature is autobiography's *transformative* power. Through this medium, people who exist somehow on the margins of mainstream America and its values have shaped self-images of their own design. Among these, blacks, pacifists, women, expatriates, homo-sexuals, artists, political dissidents, and others have described their own feelings, actions, ideas, desires, relationships, aspirations, and efforts to survive—in their own words. And their lives become available by the autobiographer's own intent, or simply by the act of publication, as models for other human beings who share certain conditions with the writer. Autobiography, at its very core, is a process of self-creation. When autobiographers are conscious of this process, they can use its power in the struggle for personal freedom. For the autobiographer, and for readers influenced by published examples of people claiming the right to define themselves, autobiography can be a revolutionary act.

An instance of this consciousness can be found among contemporary women writers, many of whom feel that what they write is not separable from their lives. For them, the first step in becoming political has consisted of each examining her own personal situation and discovering in it elements held in common with other women. Only in this way does a collection of individuals—women, or others—find its identity as a group, and then as a movement. A fictional account of a group of women's passage through this process is the subject of Marilyn French's novel, *The Women's Room* (1977), while a more general discussion is offered in Joan Cassell's (1977) ethnography of the women's movement.

Perhaps the French philosopher Simone de Beauvoir (1952) should be credited with first awakening women to the idea that the personal is also political, but the awareness has become so widespread that literary critics Julia P. Stanley and Susan J. Wolfe (Robbins) (1978) see confession as the source of an emerging feminist aesthetic in literature. They note, interestingly, that confessional literature by women has been condemned as unaesthetic by the male guardians of high culture. Perhaps the reason is that traditionally the writing of women has been very immediate in describing the intimate details of daily events and domestic emotions, while the male-made canons of art demand, instead, "proper" distance. As Thomas J. Scheff (personal communication; also see 1977, 1979) suggests, however, the traditional style of women is probably closer to what he would consider a proper aesthetic distance—that is, a healthy distance that permits the expression of vital emotions. Men's writing is "overdistanced," Scheff says, because it represses the expression of certain emotions, such as fear and grief, which women in their writing acknowledge. On the other hand, women do with anger what men do with fear and grief (express it after it's already too late), and in general *their* writing would have to be considered "overdistanced" with respect to the catharsis of anger and certain other feelings (although angry women characters experienced a renaissance in the 1970s, as French's book shows). As Stanley and Wolfe (Robbins) write:

> The women of the 20th century who write speak out of a tradition of invisibility, a tradition of the closely guarded, personal, revelatory language of diaries and journals. Our style, therefore, does not conform to the male style we have been taught to regard as "literary" and "correct." Use of the term "confessional" to automatically condemn any work of art reflects the literary tradition of a male-dominated culture which perpetuates a false dichotomy between our lives and our art. The so-called "confessional style," the voice of women for centuries, is only said to be non-literature when written by women, because we are said to be using it emotionally, not artistically. When, however, an Augustine or a Rousseau writes what he calls "confessions," he is said to be exploring the profundities of the "human condition." Such is the critical universe of discourse created within patriarchal culture. (1978:62)

The spirit of locating one's own place in the scheme of things and working openly from that place characterizes the revolutionary writings of theologian Mary Daly (1973, 1975, 1978). In a review of her own

writing as a "radical Catholic" before her dramatic change in consciousness to "postchristian feminist," Daly discovers that she had kept herself
from making a personal statement in her early work because she used
language that created an illusion of distance. "Flipping through a few
pages," Daly writes, "I noted that the author had used the rather
pompous editorial 'we' instead of 'I' and had written 'they' to refer to
women, instead of 'we.' Why did she say 'we' when she meant 'I' and
'they' when she meant 'we'?" (Daly 1975:6). Presumably, this sense of
disassociation in the earlier work from what she now feels to be truly her
self is so strong that Daly refers to herself in the past as "the author,"
because that former persona now feels inauthentic.

In the realm of cross-cultural experience, one of anthropology's
more usual concerns, Maxine Hong Kingston's autobiographical novel
The Woman Warrior: Memoirs of a Girlhood Among Ghosts (1976) offers an
unparalleled personal account of a Chinese-American woman who
forges her own identity against tremendous resistance. The girl in this
story identifies with the heroes in the Chinese folktales of vengeance and
mastery that her mother—once a village doctor, now, in this country, a
laundress—recounts. Taking on the persona of a woman warrior, the
girl performs great deeds in her imagination, saving whole villages from
destruction, and these victories give sustenance to her real-life battle
against the elements of a patriarchal culture that might teach her to
despise herself because she was born female. The progress is something
like the triumph of Joan of Arc, who by listening to her inner voices, and
by daring to snatch some of the powers her society insisted only men
should wield, transformed herself from a simple peasant girl into a
brilliant military leader. But if Saint Joan was later put to the stake for
making this transformation, perhaps it is an encouraging lesson of our
times that Kingston (or her protagonist) could pull it off and live to tell
her own tale.

The idea that autobiography is a creative act, rich with symbolic
possibilities and full of potential for self-discovery and transformation,
is explored in many critical studies, particularly in the field of literature.
In André Maurois's (1929) book of Oxford lectures on biography can be
found a chapter on autobiography that is as apt today as when it was
written. Among the newer works that readers may find stimulating and
insightful are James Olney's *Metaphors of Self* (1972) and a collection
edited by him, *Autobiography: Essays Theoretical and Critical* (1980). Others

are Thomas Cooley's *Educated Lives* (1976), M.K. Blasing's *The Art of Life* (1977), Elizabeth Bruss's *Autobiographical Acts* (1976), Roy Pascal's *Design and Truth in Autobiography* (1960), Roger J. Porter and H.R. Wolf's excellent sampler and text, *The Voice Within: Reading and Writing Autobiography* (1973), and for an examination of the philosophical foundations on which personal wisdom rests, William Earle's *The Autobiographical Consciousness* (1972).

On the ways in which the autobiographies of women are distinctive from those written by men, the collection of articles edited by Estelle C. Jelinek, *Women's Autobiography: Essays in Criticism* (1980), is essential reading. See also Grace Stewart's *A New Mythos: The Novel of the Artist as Heroine 1877–1977* (1979), which examines the innovation by women writers of myths that lend support to their creative efforts outside the sanctioned domestic sphere and fill the gaps left by the classical myths male artists have appropriated for their own ends.

Again, this list must be only partial. But it can serve nonetheless as a guide to further exploration of the terrain in which the self-transformation of autobiography takes place.

Biography: Voices in Harmony

Compared to the solo voice of an autobiography, what we often hear in a biography is two voices singing different versions of the same melody. A biography is indeed a report by one person about the life of another, but the writer usually relies as much as possible on the subject's own expressive statements and deeds as the point of departure for interpretation. The result is that the writer and subject, not being the same person, quite understandably have different things to say about the same set of facts and issues. Because of this variance in perspective, readers cannot make inferences about the experiences of the subject of a biography as reliably as they might when subjects are writing about themselves, as Allport (1942) explains. The biographer's intervening role has to be taken into account, just as it must be considered when using anthropological life histories that have been presented as "auto-biographies" of non-Westerners. In fact, the difficulty of distinguishing between autobiographies and biographies of non-Western informants, especially in the early days of this type of research, was responsible for the categorizing of both genres together under the new term "life history."

As Clyde Kluckhohn, in *The Use of Personal Documents in Anthropology*, explains:

> The lumping of "biographical" and "autobiographical" documents is dictated by the circumstance that it is often a highly arbitrary decision as to which category is the appropriate one. When a life history has been obtained through an interpreter or written down by an informant whose mastery of the English language is uncertain, when the stories came from cultures where the sensitivity to chronological sequence is much less highly developed than our own, when stylistic repetitions or cultural clichés are felt by the European or American as hampering the effectiveness of the document, editors have frequently re-arranged, omitted, modified to much more than a trifling extent. Many documents that are entitled "auto-biographies" could more correctly have been called "biographies based upon materials provided by the subject." (1945:81–82)

At the time Kluckhohn was writing these remarks, much of the material which could qualify as a life history for anthropological purposes was collected by writers outside the profession. Since the circumstances were not usually described under which even the life histories by anthropologists were collected, the lumping together of autobiographies and biographies was quite appropriate. Yet as the literature has grown, more anthropologists have become explicitly concerned with reflexive issues. For many, our methods, motives, and the assumptions underlying our work have moved to the forefront of interest—as is indicated by such work as Nash and Wintrob's (1972) article on the emergence of self-consciousness in anthropology and Honigmann's (1976) article on the use by ethnographers in the field of personal resources apart from the formal methods of their discipline. Not only do professionals seem more aware than ever of the role played in ethnography by the unique skills and perspectives of individual researchers, but moreover their attitude toward this aspect of the research situation is shifting from one of distress about "subjective bias" to one of acceptance. In a most unusual book written from notes compiled during thirty years of research in cross-cultural psychiatry, George Devereux (1967) documents, for example, actual cases in which an investigator's unconscious reactions to emotional threat posed by a specific research situation affected the formulation of the problem, the way the data were collected, and the interpretation of results. Rather than conclude that all social-science research is therefore invalid as a result of this process (called, in Freudian psychology, "countertransference"), Devereux suggests instead that we might become more aware of the way our minds work when doing research and usefully cultivate this sensibility. A similar study of reflexivity in research appears in an article on Freud's work on the interpretation of female patients' accounts of father-daughter incest by Florence Rush (1977), who argues that Freud treated these accounts as wishes or fantasies because of his personal inability to accept them as factual. While a movement toward self-reflexive anthropology definitely is gaining momentum (see, for example, Dumont 1978; Rabinow 1977; Ruby 1977; and Scholte 1970), there has been some awareness throughout the history of the discipline that the mirror effect of members of one culture describing another culture could be incorporated into research by design. Writing a preface to a book based on life histories of high-caste Hindus by Carstairs (1958), whose childhood was spent in India, Margaret Mead remarked that "advances in the application of scientific knowledge to our understanding of man have been dependent on two developments, methods of observing other human beings and *methods of observing ourselves, as observers.* Articulateness about the observed, unrelieved by articulateness about the biases and blindnesses of the observer, gives us arid material," Mead asserts. It is material "either devoid of all meaning or so heavily weighted with unacknowledged emotions that they are meaningful only to those who share the same biases" (1958:5; emphasis added).

What this has to do with the life-history enterprise is that we may need to know more than is usually reported about how the anthropologist, as biographer, has shaped the portrait we are reading. One dimension of the portrayal lies in the style of writing adopted by the ethnographer. By utilizing the freedom and expressiveness of language that traditionally has been reserved for fiction, ethnographic writing— including, of course, life histories—can gain effectiveness in conveying the subtleties of another way of life (see Langness and Frank 1978, for a fuller discussion of the uses of ethnographic fiction; also Frank *In press*). It also may convey better the complexities of the researcher's contribution to the data. Clifford Geertz (1973:3–30) advocates the use of "thick description" in ethnography—that is, a style so well balanced between anecdote and explication that it permits us to develop our own insider's view of the events described. Such a style involves the reader in the dynamic aspect of culture—the vivid, streaming, kaleidoscopic experiences of life as it is lived. It is an alternative to impersonal devices such as the avoidance of the pronoun "I" in scholarly writing, which obscures the fact that an individual human researcher is presenting observations that, after all, are temporal and finite (Parssinen 1974, 1975). The question of why we write and whom we address is one that also should be asked more often than it is. Posing this question to himself, Vincent Crapanzano (1977a; also see 1980, which is described in the Introduction to this book) suggests that the writing of an ethnography be understood as being equally an act of self-constitution for the ethnographer and a description of the world. What Crapanzano seems to mean is that ethnographers have to put themselves back together after having faced the challenging yet also traumatic experiences of life in an alien milieu. As the ethnographer's self gets created anew to incorporate the experiences encountered in the field, the writing is addressed (at least implicitly) to significant persons in the writer's life. When the ethnographer is describing another person rather than an entire culture, then the life history may be seen as a kind of double autobiography in which two personal configurations are fused: the writer's (mainly through such elements as choice of topics and tone) and the subject's (through what is usually thought of as the content of the book). Crapanzano writes:

> The ethnographer in writing ethnography is doing more, it would seem, than making a scientific contribution or convincing others to hire, reappoint, or promote him. He is affirming an identity, subjectivity felt as a sense of self, by addressing and reifying thereby, an other. The question remains: *Who is this other, whose standpoint the ethnographer takes in his act of self-constitution?* Surely, if the contention about the multidimensionality of the other is correct, he is much more than the name to whom the ethnography is dedicated. He is more, too, than the ethnographer's professional or public audience, his spouse, his father, his mother, his mentors, or any other significant other in his personal history against whom he wishes to separate or measure himself or from whom he desires recognition. The other of ethnography is, I suggest, an essentially more complex other—a bifurcate other. He is at once the significant other of the ethnographer's own cultural world and the other of the ethnographic confrontation. The writer of ethnography writes—and creates—a double audience: the audience of his own people and the audience of those other people whom he refers to in an act of presumptive if not patronizing incorporation as "my people." The writing of ethnography— and this must have an effect upon the objectivity if not the scientific validity

of the work—is essentially a compromise formation. The ethnographer wants to reconstitute his old self—or his new professional self—through an act of writing that is addressed to the significant others within his own world. He wants, too, to address, and must inevitably address, those illiterate others of his fieldwork—not simply out of good faith, professional responsibility, integrity, guilt, irritation, resentment, hatred, or the desire to fill an obligation, but also out of a necessity to declare them worthy of having been and continuing to be that silent audience by which he identifies himself as an ethnographer and obtains his sense of self. (Crapanzano 1977a:72)

In summary, a life historian consciously attempts to accurately portray the subject of the biography. At the same time, because a document that expresses the *ethnographer's* experience in the field is involved, he or she will be shaping a self-portrait composed of attitudes taken with regard to that work. In *Tuhami: Portrait of a Moroccan* (1980), Crapanzano does explicitly document his own emotional and intellectual experiences in working with his subject and offers a double portrait, although Tuhami always remains the primary focus. In *Oscar: An Inquiry into the Nature of Sanity*, Peter Wilson (1975) uses a highly readable style of reporting incidents that also conveys the give and take between an anthropologist and the subject of a life history. (See Chapter III, in which we discuss this book in greater detail.)

The bold confrontation of the other, of which Crapanzano writes, is also faced by Miles Richardson, who shares some quite personal reminiscences in his article, "Anthropologist—The Myth Teller" (1975) in order to underscore his point that ethnographer and informant are fundamentally just two human beings who encounter each other in daily existence. Together they are facing the reality of being human and each is telling his or her version of "the human myth." Personal accounts of fieldwork such as Kenneth Read's elegant and moving book about his experiences in New Guinea, *The High Valley* (1965), also have a strong biographical element and can reveal the intense and sometimes even mystical communion of the spirit that working with informants can bring. In her more recent study of an American man of Greek descent living in Greece as an expatriate, Mary McFadden (1975) adds a threoretical focus to such descriptions of the interpersonal affinity that can occur between researcher and subject. She talks about each using empathy to understand the other's thoughts and feelings, and each finding metaphors for their relationship—in this case, "father" and "daughter"—in order to establish a sense of familiarity, reciprocity, and ease. Empathy and metaphor enable them to create a sphere of what McFadden calls "mutuality," allowing them to develop a relationship beyond their initial rapport.

The "Self" in Question

As a Western literary form, biography carries with it certain assumptions about what a person is. In an article in the journal *Biography*, Peter Nagourney (1978) writes that these cultural biases are so basic as to seem inevitable to us. We expect a biography to present a unified life through anecdotes that reveal this unity while, at the same time, demonstrating change or growth. In autobiography and biography, Westerners make a story out of a life, telling it chronologically from early childhood on, ferreting out the subject's own feelings and interpretations of events, and centering it around a moral paradigm of cause and effect. The autobiography of anthropologist Margaret Mead, *Blackberry Winter* (1975), is a fine example of biography in the traditional Western mode just outlined.

How well do the assumptions of Western biography hold for the lives of non-Western informants? In the case of Tukbaw, an adult male of the Ilongot tribe in the Philippines, the answer is that they do not hold very well (R. Rosaldo 1976). The Ilongot are economically self-sufficient dry rice cultivators and hunters of deer and wild boar. Their cultural and territorial integrity is due in part to their head-hunting forays among neighboring Christian groups. Anthropologist Renato Rosaldo chose Tukbaw as a life-history subject because of his outstanding qualities: perceptiveness in human affairs, persuasiveness as an orator, and sheer charisma. Because Tukbaw was intelligent, even gifted, *and* introspective, Rosaldo expected his narrative to reveal a person whose inner life would be intricate and deep. This expectation turned out to be a mistake. Looking for psychological depth in Tukbaw's narrative and expecting to find a confession from the inner core of Tukbaw's intimate and private being was an ethnocentric assumption. In his account, Tukbaw concerned himself instead with his public self—his role in social actions, his personal integrity, and the force of his personality, which led to the esteem in which his community held him. His autobiography did not emerge as a single narrative, nor was it told chronologically. Mainly it grew out of anecdotes shared with Rosaldo to teach him the Ilongot language. Only after their friendship and symbolic adoption of each other as "brothers" were tested and proved did Tukbaw relate the story of his life in a manner we would definitely call autobiographical. As a result, Rosaldo writes, the text of Tukbaw's narrative was profoundly shaped by the situation, the questions asked by the ethnographer, and Tukbaw's own intentions. It was structured by the very relationship between the two men. Thus Rosaldo suggests that while most anthropologists have assumed that the life history is a natural and universal narrative form, this is not the case. Placing a microphone in front of a nonliterate informant will not necessarily lead to autobiography as we know it. Rosaldo writes:

> I do not believe that members of his culture were accustomed to telling their life stories in any form, and certainly not in a way intimate, revealing, and confessional. Narratives, of course, were familiar; Tukbaw often told the tale of a hunt, of a raid, of a fishing trip. What was not familiar was that he himself should be the subject of the narrative. In terms of his own cultural lore and expectations, Tukbaw's narrative was neither appropriate nor inappropriate; it simply was an exploration of little-known cultural terrain. (R. Rosaldo 1976:122)

Similarly, in Bali, a person's public self is valued over the person's more private identities (Geertz 1973:360–411; 1979). Sometimes the most private identities are completely submerged from a Western perspective and it seems that the individual's "real self" is being eclipsed by a mere role. The Balinese, however, would say that the real self is the one that is being expressed. Each Balinese person has several names, but only one corresponds to what we would call a given name. The rest are family names, status designations, birth-order names, occupational titles, honorifics, and other references to social position. The given name is often a nonsense syllable, known by few people and rarely used. With the death of the individual this name may pass entirely out of living memory. We may consequently ask whether it is feasible to collect an autobiography or life history from a Balinese informant, or whether the biographic idiom would so distort Balinese personal experience as to make sense only to a reader with Western assumptions.

In the ethnographic encounter between an anthropologist and non-Western informant, Crapanzano (1977b) suggests that reading or hearing the finished text of the life history may not only seem foreign to the subject but may even be a shocking or alienating experience. Even when informants feel comfortable about the textual version of their life that the anthropologist writes, its content may be nevertheless something of a surprise. This is what happened when anthropologist James Spradley presented to his informant James Sewid, a Kwakiutl hereditary chief, the finished version of *Guests Never Leave Hungry* (1969), a study of bicultural adaptation. While remaining a traditional ceremonial leader, Sewid became skipper of his own fishing boat, ran a profitable business, held administrative positions in his community, became an official in the Anglican Church, and otherwise managed to keep a foot planted firmly in each of two worlds. When his life history was read back to him, Sewid accepted the story as his own and made few changes. Yet he had never thought of his life in quite that way before. "I think it is a wonderful life," he told Spradley:

> That's all I can say. I think it is a full life. I didn't realize it, I didn't think nothing of it before now. It's all come to me and I'm sure now, I was looking forward to hearing how it would sound and what it was going to be like and I'm sure it is going to be something to see. I only wish that I live another few years and then I can make another, what we have left out when the book closes, what happens in the future. (Spradley 1969:288)

Sewid's experience is not unique. Writing one's own life story is a way of creating coherence or meaning. It can be a source of great satisfaction and can be used as a therapeutic technique for people of all ages, perhaps the elderly especially (Frank 1980a). Psychologist Robert N. Butler (1968) suggests that spontaneous reminiscence or "life review" is a universal feature of old age, one that is prompted by a person's recognition of impending death and the dissolution of the self. We do not really know much, however, about the life review as a phenomenon that may operate for individuals cross-culturally. Perhaps it is an artifact of Western cultures, where the ethos of individualism, the decline of religious belief in a hereafter, and the relative isolation of the elderly may contribute to inner experiences of this type. In any case, the reminiscences of the life review are primarily flashbacks that arise involuntarily. This is something quite different from the articulated and coherent narrative of autobiography. Also different from autobiography is the flow of self-related images that spontaneously arise in one's consciousness during periods of introspection, such as the re-living of embarrassment or shame in moments of solitude, when driving alone in a car, for example (Caughey 1979). The selectivity and focus of autobiography, and the relating of one's experiences to an audience, as well as the sustained effort involved, are the factors that make life-history work a unique and satisfying kind of experience (Myerhoff 1978, 1979, 1980a, 1980b).

Some interesting comparisons between biography and fiction can be made. If biography is conceived of as the search for historically verifiable truth, it is a scholarly problem, writes Nagourney (1978). But, he says, when biography is defined as a search for the understanding of personality, it becomes an interpretive problem. Perhaps it becomes an artistic problem as well. The coherence displayed in the life of a person in biography resembles fictional characterization. Biographers as a rule find some pattern in the life of their subject or develop a vivid impression of the person that they keep in mind while writing. Generally the subject of a biography has a much more coherent, organized life than people in real life seem to experience. Biographers begin with the pattern and supplement it with anecdotal material. Otherwise, the random data of which biographical records are composed would overwhelm the reader. The results would be perplexing, and quite possibly unreadable—a chronicle at best, to apply Croce's (1959) distinction between that and history.

The late philosopher Jean-Paul Sartre discusses the identity in the mind of most people in Western cultures between the literary assumptions of biography and our practical expectations about real lives. In his own autobiography, *The Words* (1966a), Sartre describes being taken in, as a boy, by a book meant for children about the youth of famous men. In this book, everything the young Bach, the young Cervantes, or the young Raphael did could be seen as a clue to the future novelist, composer, or painter. Every childish whim, each emotion, was an intimation of genius and future greatness. It was, Sartre writes, an invitation to read lives backwards, "as God had conceived them," starting at the end and including only evidence that supports the conclusions. There is an emerging body of anthropological research that allows us to see precisely how the "self" is shaped and expressed differently in various cultures and contexts (see, for example, Briggs 1970; Levy 1973; Myers 1979; and M. Rosaldo 1980). It may be of practical importance in a wide range of fields, from education and family therapy to law enforcement and foreign policy, to see in a fresh light how varied the inner life may be when viewed cross-culturally, and how in our own culture individual character is assigned.

Are We Who We Think We Are?

The case of Doug Valpey, a life history in progress (1980) by Jim L. Turner, has become something of a landmark in mental retardation studies before the full version has even been published. For our purposes, it can illustrate the way that autobiographies are designed to confirm the conclusions held about oneself at any given time. Doug Valpey (not a pseudonym but, by choice, his real name) is a man in his mid-thirties who was raised in an impoverished home in the high desert of Southern California, the child of elderly parents, and at a fairly young age an orphan. As a young teenager, Valpey became a ward of the court and was labeled mentally retarded. At age 21, he was declared in court to be incompetent to manage his own affairs. He remained in a ward status and was placed in a board-and-care facility with other retarded adults.

In order to keep himself occupied, Doug Valpey became interested in the study of fossils. He began not only to read about them but also to start a collection of his own. Occasionally he wrote to and received answers from professors and curators in the areas of paleontology, paleobotany, geology, and marine biology. He introduced himself to these correspondents as "a mentally retarded man interested in fossils." Valpey established friendships with several academic benefactors who sent him books, specimens, and photographs. Despite his limited formal education, he spent time in libraries, where he improved his reading skills. Eventually, he was writing articles on fossils for popular magazines read by amateurs. At age 35, after nearly a year of work with Turner, Valpey was given a battery of psychological tests that turned out the profile of a well-adjusted individual having little schooling but average intelligence.

After he was deemed "normal" and not "retarded," Doug Valpey's autobiography changed. In the first version, before the reassessment, he completely identifies himself with the mentally retarded. His experiences and particular areas of competence are used by him as evidence that "we mentally retarded people can do a lot more than most people think we can." In the second version, following the reassessment, he repeatedly asserts that he was *never* retarded, that there was never anything wrong with him. Many of the anecdotes in the first version were recounted in the second, but Valpey assigned new interpretations to them. The record of skills and accomplishments that he at first used to demonstrate the ability of retarded people to perform beyond the expectations of others was now invoked as evidence for his always having known that he wasn't retarded. Entirely new disclosures were brought out, too. His interest in rocks and fossils, earlier played down as "just my hobby," was now elaborated as part of a conscious strategy to prove his competence to others.

Turner points out that each version has a characteristic theme. When he suggested to Valpey that there seem to be two quite distinct versions of his life story, one in which he appears to accept "being retarded" and another in which he claims to have known all along that "there was nothing wrong with him," the response was very interesting. The discrepancies were to be understood in terms of the futility Valpey felt at times in trying to prove that he wasn't retarded when he knew that no one would believe him. What Turner's work with Doug Valpey shows is that under certain circumstances, individuals' interpretation of themselves can be rearranged around a new theme, calling into question the very facts. Was Doug Valpey retarded or was he not? It appears that he both was and wasn't, depending on how the evidence is viewed. Not even Valpey himself seems to be entirely decided. But is this really so strange? As Jim Turner suggests (in a personal communication), don't we all have the raw capacity to be someone different from our usual selves? Perhaps many different people? Artists, actors, schizophrenics, and children have license to act out coherent versions of the many selves that individuals have the capacity to become. There is a collaborative element in personal identity—the condition that others accept us as one thing or another. It is therefore interesting to note that Doug Valpey was not able to assert that he has "nothing wrong with him" until Turner came along to provide powerful, socially approved grounds for a redefinition.

The everyday problem of resolving contradictory themes in one's life story has been investigated by sociolinguist Charlotte Linde (1978, 1980). She presents brief narratives collected from middle-class Americans about their choice of career. A professor of sociology gives the following explanation of her decision to give up an earlier interest in the theater for her present occupation:

> I think that the probability of my ending up in academia was largely a product of the fact that my father was an academic and his father was a scientist and the *values* I was raised in were *very* much academic intellectual values. So I think there's a sense in which uh it would have been extraordinarily difficult for me to have ended up in another kind of life, although I entertained that at various points. Um I thought, as adolescents without talent are prone to do, of the performing arts in various ways. Uh I was in theater for a while in high school and college and had fantasies about making that a life which were of course unrealistic. (Linde 1978:59)

How to reconcile her early interest in the performing arts with her eventual career in sociology is the problem that the speaker is attempting to resolve. Linde points out that the speaker handles the discontinuity with a number of evaluative comments that make it very clear that she knew this early interest was a mistake. The speaker puts herself in the category of adolescents with no talent, calls her ideas about making her life in the theater "fantasies," and assures the interviewer that these ideas were of course unrealistic. By distancing herself in that way from her girlhood ambition, she maintains coherence in the story of her life as one that always has been oriented toward her present academic career. Linde suggests that the need to build this kind of coherence into life stories comes from rules underlying the structure of narratives and thought in English (if not in most, or many, Indo-European languages).

Another place where retrospective "repair work" in autobiographies seems to show up very clearly is in accounts by transsexuals (Bogdan 1974) and intersexed persons (Garfinkel 1967). Transsexuals are individuals who have undergone medical treatment to change their gender. Intersexed persons, formerly referred to as "hermaphrodites," are individuals born with primary sex characteristics of both genders. In their life stories such individuals often must try to prove that they have always been predominantly of one gender rather than the other, so as to justify their position in a society that often rigidly insists that one's social role be determined by which set of genitals a person is born with. The success or failure of one's story in convincing psychiatrists and physicians that one is "really" male or female has a direct outcome in whether an intersexed person or potential transsexual will be permitted to undergo surgery that may end the agony of ambiguity. Sociologist Erving Goffman (1963) describes the interactional devices routinely used by stigmatized persons in daily life to repair what he calls "spoiled identity." Whatever one's motives may be, the urge to make coherent, socially acceptable account of ourselves is very great, no matter who we think we are.

What Is a "Life"?

There is a strange and wonderful story by Jorge Luis Borges in which a young man falls from a horse and as a result can remember every detail of his existence. Borges, a blind writer whose occupation at one time was as director of the National Library of Argentina, is often concerned in his fiction with the structures in which knowledge is catalogued in culture, in written texts, and in the mind. He writes that Funes, the young man who fell from his horse, became "determined to reduce all of his past experience to some seventy thousand recollections, which he would later define numerically." Two considerations dissuade him, however, "the thought that the task was interminable and the thought that it was useless. He knew that at the hour of his death he would scarcely have finished classifying even all the memories of his childhood" (Borges 1962:114).

Implicit in this story is a number of very interesting issues. Among them is the suggestion that consciousness of everything that happens to us would impose an unmanageable burden upon our ability to continue living. We would be totally occupied with processing the remnants of yesterday's experience, and would have no time to go on living today. Another notion raised by Borges's story is that there must be some way of characterizing a "life" as other than the sum of events that befall a person, since we do not retain a hold on everything that does happen to us. But even though there are consequently many ways in which to see ourselves at any moment, undoubtedly there is a unity of some kind that binds together an individual's life. After all, we recognize other people not just because their name remains the same, or by their physical features, which also remain consistent to a degree, but also by their character. In time, as we get to know people, they become somewhat predictable and a pattern emerges. Similarly, we can recognize the pattern that makes us familiar to ourselves.

Our memories are selective, as the famous experiments of Frederic Bartlett have shown (1967; see also Rapaport 1961; Halacy 1970; and Kamano and Drew 1961). To remember something is not just to repeat it but, as one investigator writes, "to reconstruct, even sometimes to create, to express oneself" (Cameron 1963:742). If memory is selective, then there must be a prior structure of personal identity that provides the template by which certain events are cast as images significant enough to be stored. This, at least, is Sartre's (1966b) view; and a corollary would be that our lives are something more than just the sum of events at which we are present. The question of personal identity and its relationship to memory and autobiography is approached concretely by Sartre in a number of case studies of well-known writers, among them Jean Genet.

In *Saint Genet: Actor and Martyr* (1963), Sartre tries to uncover the "fundamental project" of the poet, novelist, and playwright Jean Genet. Genet's career as a thief, pimp, and homosexual prostitute resulted in his long-term imprisonment and yet his contribution to literature made the case a *cause célèbre* of French intellectuals, Sartre among them. By "fundamental project," Sartre means the organizing principle or nexus of meanings and values that inform a person's choices. He suggests that an individual comes to identify with a fundamental project first by being labeled, by being regarded in a certain manner by society. In Genet's case it was that—as a child and an orphan adopted by prosperous farmers, property owners—he stole petty objects, was discovered, and was branded a thief. Already an outsider, he was easily cast in the role of incarnate evil by his immediate society, a contrast that justified his adopters' own proper morality. Genet's fundamental project has been to freely choose this role of evil once it was attributed to him, to claim it, elaborate on it, turn it into art, and to create his own form of spirituality.

Usually, when the pattern of a person's actions is discussed, it is spoken of as that individual's "personality." To talk instead, or in addition, about a person's "fundamental project" has certain advantages for seeing that individual's life as a whole. Rather than concentrating on the person's past actions and seeing them as having put an indelible stamp on a person's future, the concept of a fundamental project focuses on the person's need to have something to live for. (For an introduction to psychological theories and therapies that focus on finding meaning and anticipating the future, see Frankl 1963; Binswanger 1960, 1963; Boss 1963; and Spiegelberg 1972.) It is revealing that Sartre himself, upon losing the vision in his one good eye at about age 70, therefore losing the ability to write, is quoted as having said, "I have lost my reason for being" (Woodward 1980). Stories of religious conversion, too numerous to begin to cite here, are evidence that the meaning around which a person's life is organized can change. It is really *freedom* that Sartre perceives in Genet's choice of evil, and indeed Sartre's entire philosophy is a radical theory of human freedom, exploring all possible consequences. If freedom as he describes it is a universal human condition, then it remains for anthropologists to consider this possibility when attempting to understand lives in foreign contexts. A collection of essays on the concept of freedom in anthropology by David Bidney (1963) dealt mainly with political freedom. It is clear, however, that Sartre is talking about a different kind of freedom entirely—the freedom to make meaning.

The Social Ordering of Personal Experience

If no single definition of a life seems suitable, it may be because of the tremendous potential of each person to become so many things. Cross-culturally, only the barest outlines of the individual life seem to be comparable. Take, for example, the sociological perspective provided by Arnold Van Gennep (1960) on "life crises" that are points of transition between one status in life and the next in a socially ordained sequence. In *The Rites of Passage*, Van Gennep suggests that in every culture birth, puberty, marriage, and death are marked by ceremonies that have much in common with those that are performed on similar occasions in other cultures. He likens the course of the human life to the rhythms of nature, because there seems to be an underlying natural unity to the rites of passage that occur cross-culturally. Van Gennep writes:

> The life of an individual in any society is a series of passages from one age to another and from one occupation to another. . . . Thus we encounter a wide degree of general similarily among ceremonies of birth, childhood, social puberty, betrothal, marriage, pregnancy, fatherhood, initiation into religious societies, and funerals. In this respect, man's life resembles nature, from which neither the individual nor the society stands independent. The universe itself is governed by a periodicity which has repercussions on human life, with stages and transitions, movements forward, and periods of relative inactivity. (Van Gennep 1960:2–3)

In fact, the only events that definitely do take place for all persons in all cultures are birth and death. These are dictated by nature. All else may be a matter of individual choice and cultural design. In general, social life depends on ushering each generation through the specific roles of productive activity that permit the group to survive. Personal freedom having just been discussed as an approach to understanding lives, it is important also to talk about the ways in which cultures traditionally have ordered and even determined the course of personal existence. Perhaps the primary source of control has been through the sanction of rites of passage. In non-Western societies—particularly ones that were once called primitive, but that actually represent the vast bulk of human social life when considered in an historical frame—failure to fit one's ritually prescribed status could result not only in alienation for the individual, but even in death. The rites of passage are linked to gender identity, because of the basic sexual division of labor in small-scale and pre-industrial societies according to whether or not one is a bearer of children. Since it is often easiest to see how a rule works by looking at an instance of its violation, let us consider the effect on two individuals of their failure to achieve a prescribed rite of passage—the one that would define the person as an adult woman or man.

Cheporr and Lazaro are members of the Pokot tribe of Kenya, and each is intersexed, having an ambiguous sexual identity. Their life histories are presented in an article by Robert B. Edgerton (1964). The presence in each of both sets of genitals raises the question of whether, at puberty, these individuals should be initiated into adult life as a male or a female. It further raises the question of what the consequences will be for their future if they cannot be initiated as a member of either group. According to Edgerton, the birth of an intersexed child is considered a misfortune by the Pokot, and the infant itself is regarded as a freak. Despite government laws against infanticide, such children are frequently put to death. Regardless of whether female or male characteristics later predominate in those who manage to survive, they are considered *sererr* or "neuter"—a term incidentally that is a serious insult when directed toward a normal individual. The life of Edgerton's "female" informant, Cheporr, was full of difficulties, and her account poignant:

> When Cheporr was about 17 years old, many other girls of her age were being circumcised preparatory to marriage. This operation, which involves

clitoridectomy and excision of parts of the labia majora, is essential to the attainment of adult female status. But Cheporr could not be circumcised. People discussed her problem and said that she could never be a man and besides there was nothing there to circumcise as her penis had no prepuce. Although she was more a woman than a man, she could never be a real woman either; therefore, she could not be circumcised. She knew she could never be either a man or a woman. (Edgerton 1964:1292)

Although she did not have to endure the mutilation of her genitals of which female initiation consisted, Cheporr could only regret her lack of legitimate adult status. At the time of Edgerton's study, ten years after her peers were circumcised, Cheporr continued to live in her father's homestead, herding his large herd of livestock with complete responsibility for them. Upon his death, she could anticipate working for one of her brothers. She could never marry and would never be permitted to adopt children to work for her. Although attractive and intelligent, Cheporr says of her life: "I only sleep and eat and work. What else can I do? God made a mistake."

Lazaro, Edgerton's "male" informant, led an existence that was much more independent and socially esteemed because of his approximation of a male role. The Pokot are a patrilineal, patrilocal people. Although refused initiation as a man by the tribe's elders, who would not perform the ritual circumcision because his penis was too small and lacked a foreskin, Lazaro was given the normal inheritance of cattle and goats by his father. Through shrewdness and hard work, he increased his herd, sold livestock, purchased two grain shops in which he employed two men, and reinvested his profits in cattle. Not even the poorest of men, however, would sell Lazaro his daughter so that a wife might work for him and, becoming pregnant by another man, bear children that he could claim as his own. Typically, their answer to Lazaro's offer of marriage was: "I love your cattle but I cannot give you my daughter as you are not a man." Although under Pokot law Lazaro could have adopted a son to inherit his property, neither of his brothers was willing to give him one of their since they intended to divide Lazaro's property among themselves when he died.

"For a man, children are essential to prestige, power and wealth; for a woman, they are everything," writes Edgerton about Pokot society. A childless woman is said to be not even a person. Without initiation by their society into one gender role or the other, neither "male" nor "female" intersexed individuals could assume a fully adult status. Lucky perhaps to have survived at all, they had to forgo the pattern of adult existence that they as Pokots also believed to be the normal and necessary way of life. It is therefore interesting to compare the attitude of the Pokot toward the intersexed with the traditional attitude of the Navaho, another small-scale traditional society. This attitude, until recent times, has been reported as one of reverence or respect. According to W.W. Hill (1935), the birth of a *nadle* (intersexed person) to a Navaho woman was considered an indication of the family's future wealth and success. As an adult, the *nadle* generally took the role of a woman, acting as head of the family, and was given control of its property. Although they did not usually marry, these individuals were permitted to have sexual relations, as were transvestites, who are said to have been treated almost as reverently. Their consultation was sought in matters of matchmaking, curing, and disputes between the sexes. One wonders whether this tolerance of the intersexed among the Navaho is related to the high status and power of women in that society, since the Navaho are a matrilineal, matrilocal people whose supreme supernatural figures are female. This outlook is in sharp contrast with the strongly patriarchal cast of Pokot social organization. At any rate, what the contrast demonstrates for certain is that while every society emphasizes certain events and personal characteristics as normal and necessary, none are necessarily found in every culture. Even the rites of passage that traditionally have ordered the daily pattern of human existence are not definitive for the species as a whole. We may conclude that any analysis of personal freedom must take into consideration the particular rules of the social context in which the individual lives. This context and these rules become the background for understanding the choices that the individual makes.

Lives and Death

We have had to admit the difficulty of defining a life but, at the same time, would like to suggest that death may be a universal human condition against which lives everywhere are played out. One thing that every human life has in common with every other is this: certain death, and foreknowledge of that event. This is the suggestion of Martin Heidegger (1962), who in *Being and Time* proposed that our consciousness in the face of death is the fundamental human condition. (It should be pointed out that Sartre saw human consciousness in the world, itself, as the universal human condition, rather than death, which to him was "unrealizeable.") A summary of Heidegger's thought concerning human existence may be useful when trying to find a framework for actually studying lives cross-culturally, since there are certain categories of experience that are generated from this confrontation of the inevitability of our own death. Philosopher Hans Meyerhoff writes:

> The basic premise of Heidegger's analysis is that man alone among living creatures, as he grows conscious of himself, has a foreknowledge of his own death. But this insight only restates, within a secular context, what has been a commonplace in a long religious tradition. What distinguishes Heidegger, and other non-religious existentialist writers in our own day, from this tradition is not the problem they are dealing with, but (a) the conclusion that there is no escape from this inexorable human fate, and (b) that this conclusion is used as the basis for deriving all sorts of other categories believed to be characteristic of the human situation. These existentialist categories, for example, care, anxiety, freedom, choice, ambiguity, etc., are invariably placed in the context of the irreversible direction of time toward death and make sense only, if at all, when interpreted within this subjective context. (1960:67)

The temporal dimension of human life extends both forward and back, so that people not only find meaning in their past but also anticipate a future for themselves. This element of anticipation makes it impossible to experience our own existence in the world—or anyone else's—as a complete whole, not because of any imperfection in our cognitive powers but because of the structure of lives. From a Heideggerian point of view, our lives always have within them something still outstanding which has not yet become realized. He indicates, for example, that even the state of hopelessness is a mode of anticipation toward the possibilities of the future which have not yet been settled. The same anticipation is present for someone who is supposedly without illusions and claims to be "ready for anything." The perpetual uncompletedness of lives in the face of an indefinite future illuminates the problem encountered by biographers in the multiplicity of inter- pretations possible for the lives they study. No interpretation can be final, as all are contrived in view of the various potentialities inherent in a life while it is being lived.

How death is conceived in a particular society should affect the life story that a person tells. Meaning resides in both the past and the future. Especially as one grows older, the horizon of the future—death—becomes visible. One means of anticipating death and reconciling oneself with it is to create memorials for those who remain behind. In literate cultures an autobiography or life history can do this. Through a memorial, a future beyond one's own corporeal demise is anticipated and met. Will a person live on in a spirit world, perhaps to be reincarnated in another body? What will be the person's status in the afterlife? Or will the person's spark be scattered, or extinguished? Is one's immortality assured by having children, who themselves bear living issue? Such questions point to the larger frame in which lives are lived and in which biographies cross-culturally could be written.

While death in the factual, biological sense means the perishing of something that was once alive, Heidegger views death as the transition of a once living entity to the same entity still present at hand but no longer embodied. The possibilities of being with the dead, and of the dead being with us, are recognized more in cultures where ancestors and spirits are felt to exert real influence over events in the world of the living. The Pygmies reckon with the various degrees of illness, and ultimately of physical decease, by saying that someone is "hot, with fever, ill, dead, completely or absolutely dead, and finally, dead for ever" (Turnbull 1961:42). What this simple example illustrates is that even the concept of death in a physiological sense is culturally elaborated. How much more, then, the social and metaphysical senses in which death is understood? The Bena Bena of the New Guinea Highlands, with whom Langness did fieldwork, for instance, have a custom of holding funerals for the very old *before* they die. Eulogies and displays of grief are meant to assure the old people that they have been valued as members of the community. At the same time it suggests to them that they should think of departing from this world and, further, that they should not return as dissatisfied spirits to haunt the living.

Being as a Whole

When individuals can squarely face the certainty of their own death, the possibility of what Heidegger calls "being-as-a-whole" exists for them because they then can act authentically, having grasped the parameters of their freedom. Immersion in the everyday world of other people tends to level down individuality in favor of conventional values. Anxiety in the face of society's demands often holds individuals back from following the direction of their own impulses. (Here Heidegger is not talking about addictions and compulsions, but the unique set of preoccupations about which a person particularly cares.) When this direction is thwarted, in favor of an average or standard mode of being, the person lives inauthentically. And this, alas, may be the state in which most of us live. However, the existential "freedom toward death" of which Heidegger writes is within our reach, if not in everyone's grasp. One illustration can be found in Adrienne Rich's heroic poem, "Phantasia for Elvira Shatayev" (1978). In this very beautiful piece, in which the images are as crisp and decisive as the frozen snow on the mountaintop it describes, the leader of the Soviet women's climbing team who lost her life in August 1974 while ascending Lenin Peak speaks to the husband she left behind about the meaningfulness of her death, because it came while exerting her energies with her companions to their fullest potential.

It is valuable for people in our time to compare the stance of freedom toward death with the sometimes disproportionate and vicarious significance given to the lives of famous men and women in Western culture. Perhaps our fascination with these subjects of biography is that we can contemplate in their lives an apparent being-as-a-whole, whether real or illusory. This possibility for being-as-a-whole inspires us with the sense that our own lives might be focused, too, in this manner. Perhaps the recurring themes in Western culture of chance, luck, destiny, and fate have a hidden meaning, then: a desire for our lives to reveal a design that might release us from ambiguity and the painful wrestling with conventional values as we struggle to become whoever we may be. People in all cultures seem to desire, even need in order to survive, patterns that give meaning to their lives. To find those patterns that will work best for us is one of the most critical challenges of contemporary Western culture and we can use an anthropological approach to lives in order to meet it.

CHAPTER V

Ethical and Moral Concerns

This chapter explores the balance between truthful reporting about people's lives and the need to protect individuals and their communities from disturbing intrusions or harmful exposure. The use of pseudonyms and other disguises, the question of how privacy may be defined, and the problem of managing the unusual degree of researcher responsibility in life-history studies are among the issues dealt with here. It is suggested that life histories of people ordinarily not heard from can have a profoundly humanizing influence on a world divided by sectarian interests. We include an interview with a distinguished anthropologist whose biography of the King of Swaziland is such a contribution.

*I*t is well-known that outlaws are often glorified and saints made villains in journalism to create the kind of controversy that sells copies at newsstands or keeps viewers glued to the television screen. More than that, it is often the personal lives of everyday citizens that we find plastered across newspaper headlines or shown on *The Six O'Clock Report*. The public exposure of individual lives is perhaps best understood by reference to the values of a democracy in which people need to keep informed in order to guard their freedoms. It is widely felt that members of this society should not be content with generalizations or pronouncements made by scientists, moralizers, and politicians, but should judge for themselves the tenor of the times, day by day, by the most immediate measures. And it *is* important to know about the reality of the world's events as experienced directly by other people, people who by the fact of their being human share this world with us. The anthropological life history is one alternative to the rather superficial and exploitative approach to lives that is so often encountered in the commercial media.

The anthropological life history, almost by definition, implies the study of a living person. As the masses all over the globe become literate, there is every likelihood that life histories and other ethnographies will be read by the people they are about, by their communities, or, at least, by the succeeding generation. Anthropologists must consider how the documents they publish may affect these people. The exigencies of the publishing business alone demand that anthropologists be selective about what gets into print. Anthropologists must also consider how they may affect their readers as a class of people having a certain potential for action in the world. Although not every life history will be widely read, or have great impact in the public sphere, it must be recognized that some do. A classic example is Oscar Lewis's widely acclaimed book, *The Children of Sánchez* (1961), which lent support to its author's theory of a "culture of poverty." This theory, in turn, found its way into domestic policy in the United States under the administration of President John F. Kennedy (see Valentine 1968, for a review and critique of that policy). It is *not* well known that the publication of *The Children of Sánchez* created an outrage in Mexico because the one family in it appears to represent only the most impoverished and to some sensibilities shameful side of life for a stratum of Mexican society numbering in the hundreds of thousands (Paddock 1965a, 1965b, 1965c).

Informants have their own opinions about the way they would like to be treated. It is sometimes painful but imperative that anthropologists find out what these preferences are and respond to them as fully as possible. Anthropologists may have difficulty hearing Vine Deloria's (1970) scathing denunciation, for example, of the use of American Indian communities for research that furthers anthropologists' careers without likewise benefiting their informants' lives. But it is necessary to seek out legitimate criticism as well as to accept praise, and works such as Keith H. Basso's (1979) study of Western Apache attitudes toward "the Whiteman" and Simeon W. Chilungu's (1976) analysis of the use of Anglo-American research methods in the Third World are perhaps too infrequently written. One of the authors of the present book recalls (in fact, can't forget) the response of her friend on a California Indian reservation in whose home she lived while conducting ethnohistorical research for the tribe (Frank 1975, 1980b). When asked if she would tape an interview for background information on a number of topics, the friend indignantly replied, "I'm not your informer." The request for an interview was dropped there. In addition, concern for the privacy of this friend and of other women whose life stories became part of her fieldnotes resulted in the researcher's decision *not* to write up a collection of portraits that, while still rather ignorant about life in that community, she had earlier thought of publishing. The decision to abstain from or delay in publishing certain materials is an ethical option that must be kept open. At the same time, it is important to invent ways of presenting sensitive issues that do not reflect on the reputation of known individuals. One way is by writing works of ethnographic fiction (see Langness and Frank 1978, and Frank *In press*), in which composite characters and situations reveal essential truths.

Maintaining an informant's privacy, or reputation, is perhaps the most obvious ethical problem in life-history research. There can be no doubt that under certain circumstances, revealing the true identity of informants can put their jobs in jeopardy, damage family relations, stigmatize them, provoke intrusions by the public, or even bring in the law. Such circumstances formed the background to Kenneth E. Read's research for *Other Voices* (1980), an ethnography of a male homosexual bar in which appear brief portraits of the patrons, including a number of transvestites. Read is careful to change the names of his informants, the name of the tavern, and the name of the city in which it is located. As he points out, American society is still "homophobic." Events since the writing of *Other Voices*, such as the accusation and dismissal of two young black women sailors aboard the Navy ship *Norton Sound*, found "guilty of lesbian acts" (Seiler 1980; Spiegel 1980), substantiate Read's cautiousness and demonstrate that public exposure can result in serious consequences for certain categories of people or of behavior. While speculation is not strictly a part of anthropological reporting, it is quite likely that the convicted sailors will have to account for themselves in responses to these accusations for the rest of their lives, even if their conviction was not based on fact and is overturned by a higher court (see the discussion of the coherence of life stories in Chapter IV).

In the sections that follow, we will first look in greater detail at this important issue—privacy—as it relates to life-history research in this and other cultures. But the effect of life-history research on informants by no means stops with this issue. The very relationship that develops in the collaborative life history enterprise is an area for ethical consideration. Life historians often cannot help intervening in the lives of those they write about. Some of the more subtle aspects of this intervention are discussed. We then go on to address the question of whether, and how, we might choose to have a moral effect in the world by making ourselves mediums for the voices of people who should be heard.

Truth and Privacy

The problem of privacy in life-history studies goes beyond the problem of disguising the identity of informants in other kinds of ethnographic research, for the reason that the individuality of the subject is precisely the object of detailed inquiry. Therefore, it has not been uncommon for anthropologists to publish life histories in which no attempt is made to hide the informant's actual name. It is important to recognize the degree of trust that this implies. Rarely, if ever, is there a signed contract between the parties to the research stipulating the terms in which the person's life will be described. These terms are negotiated, rather, in the course of the research itself. While it has been pointed out that the subjects of anthropological research are often politically powerless, and therefore inarticulate about protesting the publication of materials regarding their lives (Barnes 1967), it still may be said that life historians in general have conducted their research with an admirable degree of integrity and accountability. By way of contrast, it may be instructive to consider a case from contemporary journalism which illustrates the rather vampirish enterprise that commercial writing about lives solely to entertain the public can be.

The case concerns singer Dolly Parton, the reluctant subject of *Dolly!*, a 275-page biography by writer Alanna Nash (1978). Nash penned the life story of the flamboyant country superstar after befriending her during a two-day interview for a cover story in *Country Music* magazine. Parton was unhappy with the article's mention of her less than smashing debut to pop music in Waco, Texas in 1977 (although Nash did place the blame on a faulty sound system rather than the singer's vocalizing). She was also offended by Nash's quoting a local reporter's comment that he imagined the singer pouting in her private tour bus because she hadn't reappeared to give her usual autographs and interviews after the Waco performance. As a result, when *Country Music* contracted Nash to do an authorized biography of Dolly Parton, the singer refused to have anything to do with it. Nash pushed ahead with an unauthorized account.

In an article in *Writer's Digest* (1979), a resourceful Alanna Nash reveals her techniques for getting uncooperative subjects to talk: Corner them at press conferences, she counsels. They can't refuse to talk there. Another trick is to get other journalists to slip in questions when they are conducting interviews, then pay them back with a credit in your book. Number Three on Nash's list is called "Make Your Failures Work for You, or How to Use the Non-Interview for Effect." It involves muscling into situations where one's presence is not wanted and describing what happens next. Here is how Number Three worked for Nash when she approached members of Dolly Parton's family for an interview in their home town of Sevierville, Tennessee:

> Mrs. Parton, standing in the middle of her living room unwrapping a roll of blue toilet paper, became enraged, screaming, "No interviews, no interviews!" Her husband, lying on the couch, tried to calm her, saying, "Now, Avie, don't be rude," but Mrs. Parton let him know he'd better not talk to me either, if he knew what was good for him. Mrs. Parton's quick temper, her pride and her stubborness are all traits inherited by her daughter. Mrs. Parton's little scene, which I included in the book, also told me a lot about how Dolly's success has affected these shy, simple people. (Nash 1979:22)

Anthropologists and other readers may wonder how Nash justifies her position as an interloper, drawing conclusions about people she knows only through the hostile response she has provoked from them. In a face-to-face confrontation with Nash, Dolly Parton accused the writer of trying to exploit her life for personal gain in money and reputation. Their dialogue says something about the mores of our society, in which entering the marketplace as a public personality may mean forfeiting the right to privacy which everyone normally expects to enjoy.

"Everybody's treatin' me like a product, wantin' to write books about me, wantin' to write my life story," Parton is quoted. "What right have you got to tell my story?"

"You're a public figure," Nash answered. "All your professional life, you've been inviting people to write about you, to pass judgment on your writing and singing. Now you don't want it."

"You're just trying to make money off me," Parton accused the writer. "Everybody is."

"I'm not doing this for money, Dolly," Nash protested. "I'm doing it for a number of reasons, but money is not one of them."

"Then you're doing it for prestige," Parton snapped back. "I may not be big now, but I'm gonna be," she explained. "I'm miles yet from where I wanna go."

"See, Dolly," Nash concluded, "this is why people are treating you like a product. You *are* a product. Don't you realize you've brought this upon yourself?" (Nash 1979:24)

By choosing to make her career as an entertainer, Dolly Parton did perhaps in some sense ask for the publicity she now receives, even as the result of unwelcome intrusions by ambitious writers. However, her situation is too often shared by others in the public eye who never really wished to be there.

As far as most *anthropological* writing is concerned, informants have a right to remain anonymous, according to the Principles of Professional Responsibility (PPR) adopted by the American Anthropological Association (1973). This right is to be respected in every instance of publishing research, except where an explicit agreement has been reached to make the informant's identity known. Those people whose lives are the object of research are to be given an understanding of the capacities of cameras, tape recorders, and other data-gathering devices.

They must be free to reject them, and some informants do make this choice. (Tukbaw, the Ilongot subject of a life history by Renato Rosaldo published in 1976, and described in Chapter IV, is one such informant.) If recording devices *are* used, the data should not be employed in any way that would threaten an informant's physical, social, or psychological well-being. Despite the best safeguards, however, an informant's right to anonymity sometimes is unintentionally compromised, as a 1976 amendment to the PPR notes—particularly in small communities where pseudonyms alone may not prevent a person from being recognized by just those people for whom the disguise is meant: family, friends, neighbors, employers, social workers, or the police.

Nothing in the literature on ethics illustrates the ineffectiveness of using pseudonyms in a small community as effectively as Barbara Harrell-Bond's experiences in studying the African professional class in Sierra Leone. At the time Harrel-Bond conducted her study, there were 754 persons with professional qualifications living and working in the country. Many were closely connected through family and marriage or were at least acquainted with each other. In the first report of her research, Harrell-Bond used a large number of case studies and verbatim accounts to document her conclusions—an excellent scientific procedure—but discovered to her horror that although she had attempted to conceal the identity of the individuals mentioned, almost everyone who read the material recognized immediately who was involved:

> For example, I handed one chapter to a woman to read. It contained a case study about a professional who told me that he was the illegitimate son of a retired professional person. He explained the unpleasant relationship he had had with his father's wife and the neglect he and his mother had suffered through the years. He also disclosed other personal information about his own marriage and that of his father. Halfway through the reading she told me the names of all the individuals involved and gave me even further information. (Harrell-Bond 1976:119)

Harrell-Bond was relieved that this woman was not one of the persons she had interviewed for the research, or "she might have been understandably alarmed at how much of her own personal life might soon be in print." As a result of this problem, much illustrative material had to be discarded in the final writing of Harrell-Bond's research and withheld from publication. "The rights of privacy," she states, "had to take precedence over the claims of science for well-documented data."

Sometimes the general public relentlessly pursues and identifies the people scholars write about, as was the case with Theodore Rosengarten's oral history of an 88-year-old black Alabama sharecropper, published as *All God's Dangers: The Life of Nate Shaw* (1975). In its first edition, the book noted that while the characters were real, their names except for historical figures were fictitious and that the names of places and landmarks were also changed. "Nate Shaw" had been a union man, standing up for his rights and the rights of tenant farmers like himself one December morning in 1932, when he backed up a neighbor whose livestock was about to be confiscated by a crowd of deputy sheriffs. He paid for his defiance with twelve years in jail, and his family, left to run the farm without him, suffered too. When he returned to them at age 59, he had to start all over again. Receipt of a National Book Award by *All God's Dangers* aroused the curiosity of the public regarding the identity of the narrator. A later edition notes that while changes were made to protect the privacy of the family of the principal character, "since the publication of the first edition, articles in various newspapers and magazines have identified the real Nate Shaw: He is Ned Cobb." Ned Cobb had died in the intervening period, and so the author adds that "the family of Ned Cobb, the publisher, and Theodore Rosengarten join in proudly acknowledging that Nate Shaw is the fictitious name of Ned Cobb" (Rosengarten 1975:xii).

Again, the difficulty of maintaining a disguise crops up in the life story of Vincent Swaggi (a pseudonym), whose career as a dealer in stolen property in Philadelphia is the topic of sociologist Carl Kocklars' book, *The Professional Fence* (1974). Writing this book entailed calculated risks with underworld figures and the law. For Kocklars, the main problem in deciding what to publish about Vincent Swaggi was that a professional fence is also a professional informant, or, to put it less elegantly, a "rat" or "squealer." A fence trades with the police, giving them high-quality information that is used to secure arrests and convictions and to recover stolen property. In return, the fence is guaranteed a "license" to deal in stolen goods in limited quantities. Vincent Swaggi's life story could make the Philadelphia police look bad, forcing them to apprehend him should the public, unsophisticated about real police methods, become aroused. Moreover, Swaggi, who in private liked to call himself "the greatest undercover agent in the country," was reluctant to implicate himself as someone who had betrayed his associates in crime. Kocklars knew that no fence can operate for very long without becoming a police informant. If the book was going to provide an accurate account of the realities of the fencing business, Vincent Swaggi's informant activities would have to be made explicit. But, to quote Swaggi: "You tell about that an' I'll have every gang in the country gunnin' for me." As a writer, Kocklars compromised by leaving out material directly related to Swaggi as a police informant, alluding instead to the exploits of Jonathan Wild, who not only was the greatest fence in history but the genius behind the modern police system.

Unpredictably, Vincent Swaggi blew his own cover. Unable to resist a little advance publicity for his book, he told everybody—judges, lawyers, politicians, prosecutors, thieves, hustlers, and most of his good customers—about the forthcoming life history. The full-page review of *The Professional Fence* that appeared in the *New York Times Book Review* began with a description of Swaggi's store that included details Kocklars hadn't even mentioned in the book. Swaggi began to carry the book in his store and gave away autographed copies. He refused, however, to appear on the *Today* show, or on *Tomorrow*, and he turned down an offer from David Susskind—all for reasons Kocklars says he is not yet prepared to speculate about in print. The tremendous popularity of *The Professional Fence* offset occasional outcries from Philadelphia's respectable citizenry, and no legal action against Swaggi ensued.

When Swaggi died of cancer about a year after the book's appearance in print, hundreds flocked to his wake. Fewer than one in ten signed the guest book—a reminder that although Swaggi himself went public with impunity, others were cautious about guilt by association. Even after Swaggi's death, Kocklars maintained a commitment regarding his friend Vincent's reputation and its effect on the well-being of the Swaggi family:

> In January I received a call from an investigative reporter of the *Philadelphia Bulletin*. He said that he had been assigned to do a story on *The Professional Fence* and asked if it might be possible to meet Vincent. I told him that Vincent had died, and he said that he wanted to do the story anyway. I told him no again, explaining that, like him, I had a responsibility to keep my sources confidential and that the family would not appreciate such a story.

He said that such a story would help sell more books, and I told him to go fuck himself and hung up. I then called Vincent's daughter, who was now running the store, to tip her off to the fact that the reporter was nosing around. Two days later the reporter called me back. He had talked to the police, had Vincent's criminal record, his obituary, and half a dozen stories that his police source had given him. I asked him how much a suit against the *Bulletin* would bring if he had the wrong person, gave him the same advice that I gave him on the first call, and phoned Vincent's daughter again. The following day he arrived at the store with a photographer, and Vincent's brother gladly showed them around. He took pictures of the store, Vincent's office, and some of the decorations there—the picture of Mayor Frank Rizzo, the award from the American Legion as the local post's man of the year, Vincent's green fedora that the family had decided to leave exactly where Vincent had left it. These photos and a three-page story appeared in the *Bulletin* on Sunday, February 29, 1976, a little more than five years after I first met Vincent. The story was romantic, a glorification of Vincent's criminal career. The family was not offended. (Kocklars 1977:216)

It is important to realize that while anonymity is desirable in much anthropological research (see Barnes 1979; Colvard 1967), many life-history informants *want* to use their actual names. Sometimes these are marginal individuals who by setting their own stamp on the life-history written about them make a statement to the world, offering testimony, or bearing witness, about the events that shaped their lives. This has been the case in much of the life-history work that has been done with the disabled. A portrait of "Fred Barnett" was one of three detailed cases of mentally retarded adults living in the community in Robert B. Edgerton's book, *The Cloak of Competence* (1967:41–57). When the book went to press, the real "Fred Barnett," Ted Barrett, was angry that his story appeared under a pseudonym. This concealment was rectified in subsequent research conducted with Ted by Edgerton's associates. They write:

We must not ignore the impact which the construction and dissemination of a retarded individual's life history may have on him or herself. After all our scientific justification for the proliferation of these histories, we feel there is a compelling argument for the life story affording some retarded individuals a monumental opportunity to entertain, engage in, and identify with the process of making their own worthwhile contribution to a literature of direct bearing on their future. Indeed, despite ethical arguments for the protection of subjects' privacy, we find it a compelling fact that Ted Barrett insists we no longer use his pseudonym and we honor his story by not disguising his name. We are made very aware of how committed Ted has become, and how urgently we feel about the task of making his, and our, unique contribution. (Whittemore, Koegel, and Langness 1980:25)

Similarly, Doug Valpey, subject of a life history by Jim L. Turner (1980) which describes how he lived as a retarded man until age 35 when he was declared to be of average intelligence, also preferred to use his real name in the published research. Finally, in Gelya Frank's (1981) life history of Diane Fields, a woman who is a "congenital amputee," the subject also wished to use her real name, and this request was complied with, although the researcher felt compelled to jettison certain materials reflecting on living members of the family (Frank 1981; also Frank 1979b; and Frank, *In press*, a short story based on the life-history materials). Having been born with neither legs nor arms, except for short stumps, Diane Fields' identity could scarcely be disguised anyway—there are just too few people who look like her. Sometimes it is necessary to choose to withhold certain data that may conceivably injure life-history subjects despite their desire to tell all. Researchers also should protect themselves from becoming targets for possible legal action by others mentioned. Yet it seems important to emphasize that life-history work is predicated on describing the reality experienced not by ourselves, the researchers, but by our informants. These are fundamentally *their* stories, even if we happen to also think of them as our research.

Are there any general rules about what should be considered private to an individual who is the subject of life-history research? Americans seem to feel that theirs is the right to know the truth about everything. It is one of the unwritten freedoms associated with the Bill of Rights guarantee of freedom of speech and freedom of the press. All of the social sciences—economics, political science, sociology, and psychology as well as anthropology—study the personal behavior of individuals alone and in groups. All publish information that is private to those men, women, and children. The Panel on Privacy and Behavioral Research (1967) defines the right to privacy as the individual's prerogative to choose how much of his or her thoughts, feelings and personal life to share with others. The decision about what to disclose, and when, is situational:

Actually, what is private varies for each person and from day to day and setting to setting. Indeed, the very core of the concept is the right of each individual to determine for himself in each particular setting or compartment of his life how much of his many-faceted beliefs, attitudes, and behavior he chooses to disclose. Every person lives in several different worlds, and in each his mode of response may—indeed, must be different. The roles of father, husband, clerk, good neighbor, union leader, school board chairman, candidate for office, solicitor of funds for the local church, call for different responses. The right to privacy includes the freedom to live in each of these different roles without having his performance and aspirations in one context placed in another without permission. (Panel on Privacy and Behavioral Research 1967: 8–9)

Thus the Panel concludes that "any general injunction against study of a specific area of behavior wholly misses the essence of privacy; it fails to protect some people from being exposed in ways that are most upsetting to them while shielding others who are quite willing to reveal information." It is necessary therefore, to work closely with life-history informants to secure their explicit approval for the published account, as did Leo Simmons, for example, in his classic life history of a Hopi Indian, *Sun Chief* (1942:7). It is a technique also used by Elizabeth Bott (1957:47) in her study of urban family life in London. Bott asked two of the couples who were informants for her research to go over her materials with her and found that this procedure resulted, among other things, in *more* confidential material becoming available for publication. This process may make most sense where informants are already sophisticated about the purposes of research and the consequences of appearing in print. But, as J.A. Barnes (1967) remarks, "The process may well sharpen the understanding of the investigator as well as reassure the informant."

The sociologist Georg Simmel (1950) argued that every culture must have some concept of privacy because in every society individuals have certain roles to play with particular categories of people. Thus individuals have to screen their reactions and behavior from some people on some occasions. "Shame" and "respect" regulate relations in all cultures. Degrees of social distance are expressed both spatially and linguistically—by the style of speech, terms of address, content, and amount of interaction. *How* all this is done depends on the culture. To take a most graphic example, Tuareg men in North Africa constantly wear veils that cover the entire face except for the eyes. The veil is worn even when eating or smoking a cigarette. In the familiar company of comrades or with total strangers such as anthropologist Robert F. Murphy (1964), who describes this aspect of Tuareg life, the veil may be worn relatively loose. But when men interact with their parents-in-law, the veil is drawn high and taut, making a narrow slit that obscures the eyes almost entirely. Because of the tribe's practice of in-marrying while reckoning descent bilaterally, it is virtually impossible for a man to get far enough away from his relatives by marriage to show them proper respect. Since Tuareg relationships are fraught with tensions because the lines are blurred between kin by blood and kin by marriage—the categories requiring different attitudes—the veil creates a sphere of privacy that can be adjusted to each situation. To take another instance, reported by Barnes (1967), individuals in Britain keep secret the details of their income and expenditures. Income tax returns are well guarded and after a number of years burned, never becoming part of the public record. Yet in Norway, a country not so far away, details of income and tax assessments for each individual are published yearly. In rural areas of that country, court cases and accidents are reported anonymously, while in Britain that sort of news is public fare.

Some anthropologists take the point of view that "personal tact, honesty, choice of friendships, and emotional and intellectual involvement" are strictly a private matter best left to the researcher's discretion (Fabian 1971). Still, an anthropologist cannot always easily distinguish between between strictly private matters and those that should be published. In participant observation, everything is new, everything interesting, and everything potentially useful as data (Kloos 1971). Therefore, without going so far as to suggest that we legislate morality, the guidelines established by the Principles of Professional Responsibility may be worth remembering. Simply stated, ethnographic data should not be acquired secretly, nor published without a subject's consent, no matter how remote the possibility seems that it might cause harm. Moreover, an informant's agreement to divulge certain information is not a license to publish other kinds of data revealed in the process. It is an uncomfortable fact that any ethical stance rests on an underlying set of values about which not all people necessarily agree. Therefore the difficulty of applying ethical standards to research jumps an order of magnitude when yet another culture is involved. In these cases more thought, not less, should be given to deciding what to print.

Life-History Research and Observer Intervention

Much has been written about the ambiguity of the researcher's role as perceived by informants in the field and about the difficulties or even desirability of maintaining detachment and objectivity. Often the relevant question in participant observation is not whether anthropologists should intervene in the lives of their informants, but when and how. Even an anthropologist's choice *not* to act can sometimes have important consequences. In life-history work, this situation is exaggerated, as the bond between researcher and informant is perhaps unique in its strength and duration. Retrospective accounts by anthropologists of their own careers often describe in considerable detail the ethical and moral dilemmas of participant observation. Among the best of these are Hortense Powdermaker's *Stranger and Friend* (1966) and Rosalie H. Wax's *Doing Fieldwork* (1971). Such dilemmas sometimes arise from the unexpressed expectations that researchers and informants have of each other as a result of inequalities in status and power between Europeans and "natives" (Edgerton 1965). Each starts out with stereotypes of the other that are the accumulated heritage of relations between their two peoples. Often they try to prove that *they* are different— Europeans that they are not exploitative, "natives" that they are not manipulative and unreliable. Mutual testing may take place in which both parties end up disillusioned because the stereotypes fulfill themselves prophetically in an atmosphere of basic mistrust between races, cultures, or classes.

The harboring of unexpressed expectations, conscious or unconscious, is a part of the life-history research situation that perhaps has not been explored enough. Sometimes expectations are merely hinted, and it takes a trained sensitivity both to notice them and interpret what they mean. Cross-cultural psychologist David Gutmann (personal communication) relates a story that highlights the importance for life-history researchers of cultivating that sensitivity. The incident concerns a Mexican Indian who collaborated closely with an American scholar conducting studies of language and cognition. The informant—we will call him Carlos—was an exceptionally intelligent and capable individual, as indicated by the fact that he was often singled out for special responsibilities within his own society. Carlos's relationship with the anthropologist was cast in the mold of patron and protégé, not uncommon for research in Latin America (also see Kelley 1978:11–14). On occasion, Carlos would refer to the anthropologist as "Papacito," a term of mixed affection and respect. The anthropologist's research relationship with Carlos was close and it extended over time in many varied settings. The change was therefore very abrupt when the anthropologist announced one day that he was returning to the United States—without Carlos, of course—and shortly thereafter disappeared. Carlos became deeply depressed and in time exhibited symptoms of a paranoid psychosis in which he believed that his wife was sleeping with *gringo* anthropologists. Asking a friend to accompany him as a witness, he went after her one night with a machete, with the intent to kill her in the act of adultery. She was alone, however, and despite his madness Carlos was able to restrain himself from carrying out his plan.

The outcome of Carlos's marriage and derangement are not known, but certain lessons can be drawn from this story in any event. As David Gutmann analyzes it, the American researcher failed to recognize the tremendous expectations he aroused in his informant. His sudden departure was arranged without regard for Carlos's needs, needs the anthropologist himself had fostered. In general, such behavior displayed a blindness to the most basic of clinical phenomena—transference and countertransference (also see Devereux 1967). For Gutmann, Carlos's fantasy of his wife sleeping with American anthropologists can be read as a projection of Carlos's own erotic feelings toward the researcher with whom he had worked so closely for so long. One might also note that by identifying himself with his wife in the fantasy, Carlos plays out a passive and responsive "female" role not unlike his position as informant. Gutmann stresses the need for life historians to learn the rudiments of personality theory and clinical practice. He writes:

> We are too apt to play at being democratic "good guys" at the expense of our often very hungry and vulnerable informants. We think that we are being cool, and unconcerned with status; but they too often experience our transient gestures toward equality as *massive* seductions, as was the case with Carlos. Thus, it is not enough that we develop sensitivity to our informants' motives; we should also be very sensitive toward and corrective of our own. My own recommendation is that all fieldworkers in training should be supervised not only by experts in their particular discipline, but also by clinical psychologists or psychiatrists—by those practitioners who could highlight the trainee's countertransferences toward his subjects, as well as the subject's transferences toward him.

Intervention happens not only in the manner just described, but also consciously, as a result of choices that researchers are aware of making. To retarded informants, and for other handicapped or marginal people, including the poor, and sometimes the elderly, researchers may become an important link with the wider world. In the study of mildly retarded adults living in the community (Edgerton 1978), each field researcher had three to eight informants, seen roughly once every ten days, some for as long as three years, and wrote ongoing life histories in progress. Not only did they hold scheduled interviews but they were also available by phone at all hours, got to know their informants' families and friends, visited them on special occasions, provided innumerable favors and services, and often invited them into their own homes and lives. Much of this contact was volunteered because it seemed natural to the relationship that developed out of participant observation. The retarded informants, in turn, most frequently intro-duced their researchers to others as friends. But in fact each related to the researcher as a combination friend, parent, social worker, and sometimes wishfully as a boyfriend or girlfriend. For once, here was a competent adult outside of the family who expressed interest in the minute details of their daily experiences, feelings, thoughts, pleasures, and problems—someone not in authority but one who could simply provide love, understanding, and a sense that the retarded person is an acceptable human being like everybody else. The bonus was that the researcher could also be a potent resource as a liaison or intermediary with public-assistance agencies, with informants' own families, or with other normals in a position of control. Clearly, advocacy and therapy constitute intervention in the lives of the subjects, but a researcher's decision whether or not to intervene could make a difference for informants about continuing to live independently, getting a job, getting married, or avoiding being sterilized or committed to a state hospital.

The case of "Pat S." is interesting because the researcher's special relationship of advocacy and therapy was extended to all members of her family (see Frank 1980c). Shortly after Pat was included in the sample for the study, the researcher met her parents, younger brother, and younger sister. As he puts it, "an immediate spark of friendship was felt on all sides." Within a few months, the researcher was invited to strictly family get-togethers and was soon treated like a member. His opinion was solicited in all important matters concerning Pat, and although he at first avoided taking a clear-cut stand, in order to maintain a semblance of objectivity, he increasingly found that position untenable. For one thing, he could not help noticing that there was a double standard in the family, by which Pat's ability to take care of herself was monitored and judged more severely than that of the younger children. When Pat's parents expressed their concern that she never talked about moving out or getting married, the researcher was able to point out that they had not talked to her in ways that anticipated the same future they had in mind for the other children. As a result of these insights, Pat's parents began to address her differently, beginning to say things like: "Now, you watch and see how to run the washing machine [or, shop for groceries], because when you get married, or when you live on your own, you'll have to do it yourself." This seemed to make a difference not only in the expectations of Pat's parents, but in Pat's own concern with domestic skills and perhaps in her expectations for herself. Despite occasional acts of advocacy for Pat, the researcher tried to avoid directly intervening in her life, since he felt that their excellent rapport depended on his accepting Pat just the way she is, without trying to mold her behavior.

He comments that his moral obligations to Pat eventually took precedence over his anxiety that intervening in her life would compromise the objectivity of his research:

> "Maybe nobody ever will have the understanding that you have of this person and of their situation, and maybe nobody ever will be in a role to make constructive change. And if you don't grasp the opportunity, it's going to be lost. But you only feel the obligation if there *is* a close relationship. If there's not, then you don't have the same sense of obligation to do something, or to add your perspective. But it's because there's a close relationship that there's an expectation that I will be involved in these discussions (with Pat's parents), and were I not to do so, I wouldn't be upholding my part of the bargain, in *their* minds. They wouldn't ever understand it if I said, 'I can't give you my opinion. I'm supposed to be an objective bystander.' That just wouldn't cut it." (Frank 1980c:11)

The original design for the Normalization study discouraged researcher intervention unless specifically requested by a member of the sample. In a sense, Edgerton (personal communication) now finds that this rule was unrealistic. He suggests that we might consider whether or not we are under an ethical obligation to be as human as possible with informants whose damaged self-esteem requires a supportive response.

It might even be appropriate to add the responsibility to love in our principles of professional ethics with the retarded and with the disabled in general, if not with all informants.

The Idea of an Ethical Anthropology

In 1966, when Che Guevara and Tamara Bunke, code name "Tania," were reunited in Bolivia to lay the groundwork for a people's revolution, they posed as anthropologists (Henderson and Henderson 1978). A respectable interest in ethnology and archaeology had allowed Tania to mingle with Bolivia's monied elite. She was permitted to go to the interior of the country with tape recorder and study the music of the native peoples. It was a perfect cover for her revolutionary activities, and in the meantime she was able to turn her contacts with the country's rulers into assistance for her comrades. The success of Tania's pose captures the paradoxical situation that anthropologists have often found themselves in: While most anthropologists identify to some extent with "their" people—the people they study—they have also usually been sheltered by the colonial and capitalist elite of the countries in which these people live. Like it or not, they have been politically and ideologically allied with the ruling class.

It was Kathleen Gough who coined the epithet for anthropology as "the child of imperialism" (1968). It was argued then and still is true that whom we study (and don't study), whom we work for, what theories we use, and what purposes our research is put to are all ethical issues that the individual anthropologist must take responsibility for before going into the field (Jorgensen 1971). As Gerald Berreman (1968) has pointed out, we can no longer consider native peoples our "subjects" (in both senses of the word), but must recognize that they are partners whose cooperation is to be enlisted, not coerced. For Margaret Mead—writing in 1969 that "Anthropological research does not have subjects. We work with informants in an atmosphere of trust and mutual respect"—such cooperation *defines* the discipline.

If anthropology has made an impact on the modern consciousness, it has been to supply the concept of "cultures" and of cultural relativism. The term was used for this concept by Franz Boas, mentor of Margaret Mead, Alfred Kroeber, Edward Sapir, Ruth Benedict, and scores of other first-rank anthropologists of that time. What Boas did was to decapitalize the word "Culture" (from the German *Kultur*), a word which had referred to a Western ideal, and apply it in the plural to the various ways of life that the peoples of the world have created, each in relation to its environment (Stocking 1968). Implied in the term "cultures" is the integrity of each particular ethnic adaptation and the respect that must be acknowledged toward each people. Among the contradictions of contemporary geopolitics, not least is the paradox of nationhood itself, when nationhood is identified with the ethnicity of the ruling class (as it is in the United States and practically everywhere else). Perhaps it is näive to put it so simply, but there is just not enough land and resources to enable fashioning nations for all the ethnic groups that feel they require the dubious security of political autonomy within a bounded territory. The result is often the desperate battle for power of justifiable cause against justifiable cause, culture against culture, even when—to an outsider—ethnic differences may seem so slight as to be puzzling. (For a theoretical perspective on the perception of ethnic distinctions in a foreign context, see Moerman 1974.)

Political and economic repression, torture, genocide, and holocaust are an everyday reality in the human community. The Nazi concentration camps and the massacre of defenseless citizens (such as the Russian Jews at Babi Yar by the German forces during World War II) have been identified as *the* holocaust of the twentieth century. But no less of a holocaust was the liquidation of Ugandans—black and white—under the deposed dictator Idi Amin (on the starvation of the Ik tribe, see Turnbull 1972). The terror and destruction rained upon the Vietnamese and Cambodian peoples by the French in the 1950s and the Americans in the two decades that followed are horrors burned into the memory of many who saw them enacted on their color television. Most people are not aware that today the Indians of Brazil—the Yąnomamö (Chagnon 1968) and other tribes—are being systematically exterminated just as whole populations of Indians in the United States were killed and driven from their lands by white settlers until quite recent times (Davis 1977; Indigena 1974; Ramos and Taylor 1979). And despite the victory of black Rhodesians in reclaiming their country and renaming it Zimbabwe, the murder of black journalist Steve Biko in a South African jail is a reminder of the blight that the apartheid regimes have been and continue to be.

Writer Nadine Gordimer (1979:117) has described the bourgeois fate as "to eat without hunger, mate without desire." Most likely, of those who read this book few will have themselves, in their own lifetime, been oppressed to the point of possible annihilation. Listening to the voice of those who have struggled for the simple right to exist is critical for a humanity that professes the desire to live in peace. Biographies usually take as their subject the life of some already distinguished personage, someone whom the public already knows. The anthropological life history and the other personal accounts that anthropologists collect and study most often make ordinary individuals, from backgrounds exotic or obscure, intelligible to other people. Cutting across cultural and political ideologies, they reveal what is essential about the human condition, just as good films and novels will do. To fail to understand another person's life story is, in general, to reject one's own humanity. Whether recorded in the extremity of personal or cultural annihilation, or in the midst of joy and productivity, the anthropological life history offers a positive moral opportunity to pass on stories that might otherwise never be told. For those who are bearers of a tradition, the opportunity to tell their story can be a gift: reassurance that they are indeed still alive, that their voices will be heard, and that their cultures can survive. It is a gift of equal importance for those generations to come who will take up that tradition and shape it to their own needs as the future unfolds.

The Voices of Small Heroes

Miles Richardson (1975) has suggested calling anthropologists "The Myth Tellers," since their job is to collaborate with other people to tell the human story. Barbara Myerhoff (1978:272) has proposed renaming our species "Homo narrans," the storyteller. By describing lives in their plainness and their depth, their routineness and their moments of exaltation, we recreate the human experience that has permitted our species to survive. This is exactly what Myerhoff discovered when working with a community of elderly and forgotten Jews in Venice, California—work that led to the profoundly moving book *Number Our Days* (1978) which, with producer Lynn Littman, was made into a documentary of the same name that won an Academy Award. The men and women interviewed by Myerhoff had escaped from Eastern Europe, particularly from Russia and Poland, while the Czar still reigned. The great persecutions of their own time were the *pogroms* carried out against them by the army's mounted Cossacks. Safe in America during the 1930s and 1940s, they watched from afar the destruction of their remaining families, their homes, and their culture when the Nazis seized power. Shmuel, one of the Venice elders who patiently tutored Myerhoff in the folkways of this vanishing culture, described the burden of remembering his childhood town in Poland in light of his knowledge that under Hitler's occupation his people and their way of life were destroyed: "It is not the worst thing that can happen for a man to grow old and die," Shmuel explained. "For myself, growing old would be altogether a different thing if that little town was there still."

> So in my life, I carry with me everything—all those people, all those places, I carry them around until my shoulders bend. I can see the old rabbi, the workers pulling their wagons, the man carrying his baby tied to his back, walking up from the Vistula, no money, no house, nothing to feed his child . . . . Even with all that poverty and suffering, it would be enough if the place remained; even old men like me, ending their days, would find it enough. But when I come back from those stories and remember the way they lived is gone forever, wiped out like you would erase a line of writing, then it means another thing altogether for me to accept leaving this life. If my life goes now, it means nothing. But if my life goes, with my memories, and all that is lost, that is something else to bear. (Myerhoff 1978:73–74)

Is it possible that anyone who hears and responds to what Shmuel has to say about his experiences could fail to respond similarly to the reminiscences of Palestinian exile Fawaz Turki (1974), which follow? As a child, in 1948, Turki left Haifa, Palestine—now Haifa, Israel—for a refugee camp in Beirut, where he grew up as a stateless person. He recalls sitting at that camp, perched at the edge of the desert between the city and its airport, with a crowd of people, mothers and fathers and aunts and grandparents and young wives and children, to listen to the radio at exactly three o'clock every day when the voice over the Israeli radio station would announce The Messages: " 'From Abu Sharef, and Jameela, Sami and Kamal in Haifa,' the words would come across the air. 'To our Leila and her husband Fouad. Are you in Lebanon? We are well.' A few moments' pause, then: 'From Abu and Um Shihadi, and Sofia and Osama to Abu Adib and his family. Is Anton with you? We are worried.' The dispassionate voice continues: "From Ibrahim Shawki to

his wife Zamzam. I have moved to Jaffa. Your father is safe with us.' "
(Turki 1974:9) Each day for an hour, the displaced and dispossessed
would wait for word that members of their families had survived a war
they neither understood, wanted, nor initiated.

It should be noted that Shmuel, a philosopher, was not an advocate
of Zionism—the identification of a homeland in Palestine with a Jewish
nation, although most of the other Venice elders were fervent supporters
of Israel as a refuge for their shattered people. Could anything be more
ironic than the parallel between the plaint of Shmuel, the dispossessed
Jew, and that of Turki, the dispossessed Palestinian, in describing his
father's memories and his own?

> My father died burdened with question marks from his past that he
> carried around him like a tired beast of burden pulling at a heavy cart. I am
> beginning to acquire a past of my own that is itself getting onerous.
> (1974:151)

It is unlikely, given the political contradictions we have been handed,
that empathy alone can resolve war into peace. But at least we can refuse
to be faceless stereotypes to each other. Being these is what permits
brutality to take place unchecked and shifts conflicts between oppressors
and victims to conflicts among the victims themselves.

The strictly ethical problems of anthropological biography—informed
consent, protection of sources, invasion of privacy, exploitation of the
lives of the less powerful, and so on—have been dealt with by
anthropologists in some of the more general texts. One can look at the
excellent collections of essays in the edited volumes by Rynkiewich and
Spradley (1976), Sjoberg (1971), and Wax and Cassell (1979), as well as
the text by Diener and Crandall (1978). Books are also available that
inform writers how to best protect their own interests against possible
legal action when writing about real persons, living or dead, in
biography or fiction (Polking and Meranus 1978). As anthropologist
Joan Cassell (1978) has written, a simple risk/benefit model such as the
federal government uses to evaluate medical research with human
subjects is not really appropriate to the social sciences. Because
biographers, autobiographers, novelists, and oral historians can pass on
a living tradition to the future, the positive moral possibilities for this
work are considerable. Ordinary people can be seen as the small heroes
they often are and may be taken as the teachers they can be. The creation

of a legacy from the past to a viable future can be done in a spirit of cooperation and mutual respect, without violating the privacy or integrity of their lives.

A Portrait: One of the Last of the Great African Kings

Sobhuza II, "Lion" and King of Swaziland, has been called one of the last of the great traditional rulers in Africa. When he is gone, an era in the history of that continent will have ended. One of the most remarkable life histories ever to be written by an anthropologist is Hilda Kuper's study of this man whom she has known for over forty years. Written with the advice and consent of a distinguished committee of Swazi scholars and statesmen appointed especially to assist in the preparation of this book, *Sobhuza II, Ngwenyama and King of Swaziland: The Story of an Hereditary Ruler and His Country* (1978) is a work of tremendous scholarship, intelligence, and warmth. It also happens to exemplify perhaps the best of the ethical practices and moral concerns that an anthropologist can bring to such a task. Many of the issues faced by Kuper in the preparation of this biography are ones we have discussed in the present chapter: there is the careful selection of which materials to publish, always weighed with their meaningfulness to the Swazi people in mind. There is her sense of personal obligation to these people, who had given her their friendship and trust, as well as a firm professional and academic commitment to completing what became an increasingly arduous task. There is the concern for protecting the private lives of her informants from undue public exposure. And, perhaps most striking in this biography and in the interview with Hilda Kuper which follows, there is a keen insight into the political implications of her research and awareness of the opportunity to be effective within a wider context.

Before turning to the interview, some background concerning the Swazi situation and Hilda Kuper's relationship with the Swazi people will be helpful. Professor Emeritus at the University of California, Los Angeles, Hilda Kuper was born in Rhodesia and studied anthropology at the London School of Economics. She first visited the Swazi in 1934 with her teacher, Bronislaw Malinowski. Introduced to the Swazi people by Sobhuza, whom she had met at a conference on education in Johannesburg the year before, Kuper was lodged with Sobhuza's mother, Lomawa, at her royal village. Called "laBima" (not yet married

to Leo Kuper, her maiden name was Beemer), Kuper stayed two years
among these cordial people, whose trust she eventually earned to the
extent that she came to be referred to no longer as *umlumbi*, a white, but
umuntu, a person. Many subsequent visits and the writing of several
sympathetic and insightful books on the Swazi brought her a unique
position of friendship, affection, and respect. Among these works are:
two full-length ethnographies, *An African Aristocracy: Rank among the Swazi*
(1947a) and *The Uniform of Colour* (1947b); a monograph, *The Swazi: A South
African Kingdom* (1963); a novel, *Bite of Hunger* (1965); a play, *A Witch in My
Heart* (1970); and numerous short stories and scholarly articles. *A Witch
in My Heart* has been translated into Zulu, the language used in Swazi
schools, where it has become a standard textbook. First performed by
African students at the University of Natal, the play has since appeared
on Swazi national television with an African cast. Royalties from this
play and from *Sobhuza II* have been deposited in funds for the Swazi
people, mainly for scholarships. In 1967, when Swaziland was about to
become independent of colonial rule, Hilda Kuper requested permission to become a citizen by *khonta* (the offer of traditional allegiance). In
1970 this request was granted by the King himself although she did not
meet the qualifications of residence written into the constitution.

The biography of Sobhuza II was undertaken by Hilda Kuper at the
request of the Swazi government and it was only after much soul-
searching that she at last accepted the assignment, knowing what would
be demanded of her. This would be nothing less than an official history
of the Swazi nation through the person of the King—an account of the
way in which this tiny nation, landlocked between the Union of South
Africa and Mozambique, has been able to negotiate its way from being
a dominated colonial territory to becoming an independent constitutional monarchy, under the leadership of Sobhuza building on the
efforts of his predecessors. Through political shrewdness, sheer per-
sistence, and the strength of the traditional institutions of their nation,
the Swazi people preserved a strong identity during the long period of
colonial rule. Central among the traditional institutions is a dual
sovereignty (the King and the Queen Mother), which binds together the
various clans and which is annually revitalized in the *Ncwala*, or ritual of
kingship. Sobhuza II has been able to remain Africa's longest-reigning
living king, counting the years when Swaziland's colonial rulers refused
to accord him this proper title, designating him "Paramount Chief"
instead. In the colonial period, the Swazi system with its checks and

balances was undermined and the decisions of the king and council were subjected to the authority of an agent of the British monarch. Sobhuza's clan, the Dlamini, was thrust into disproportionate prominence. At the same time, the role of the Queen Mother in decision making—a role as necessary as the King's—was virtually ignored. Yet the Swazi tenaciously, if surreptitiously, maintained Sobhuza's kingship. Thus, in ceremonies when Britain's High Commissioner appeared with Sobhuza in public, the Swazi people shouted *Bayethe!*, the royal praise, but only when the two men stood together. The High Commissioner was allowed to believe that the salute was meant for himself as representative of the British king, but it was in fact for Sobhuza, who in those years was forbidden to be hailed by his rightful title.

A chronological sketch of the Swazi struggle to remain independent and to regain their lands is in order here, because it was this struggle, so closely allied with Sobhuza's career, that prompted the Swazi to have his biography written, both to honor the man and to set the record straight. The story begins with Mbandzeni, the grandfather of Sobhuza II, who reigned a hundred years ago, during the immensely troubled period of British and Boer conflict and expansion in South Africa. Once gold was discovered in 1882, prospectors and settlers arrived in droves. Concessionaires brought liquor, guns, cash, horses, blankets, and other of the "blessings of civilization," requesting only that the king and councilors make a cross representing their names on certain documents. They had no allegiance to the Swazi king and increasingly began to interfere with the rights of the Swazi people, stealing cattle, seizing children, moving boundary markers, and treating Swazi of all ranks with injustice and brutality.

In an effort to deal with the situation, Mbandzeni appointed a trusted white to serve as "Resident Advisor," a position created to mediate between the Swazi nation and the concessionaires. It was particularly during the 10 months of serious illness leading to Mbandzeni's death in 1889, that the holder of this post of Resident Advisor—appointed in good faith by the Swazi king—granted a prodigious number of concessions over land, minerals, and industrial development that were contrary to the customs and future interests of the Swazi people. Before his death, Mbandzeni stated publicly that the land had not been sold and that the concessionaires had only been allowed the use of it as his subjects.

Under the Swazi system, a king is required to marry many queens, linking the clans to the heart of the nation. A royal heir is customarily designated only upon the death of his father and should be chosen as much by the rank of his mother as for his own royal lineage. The Queen Mother, or *Ndlovukazi* ("Lady Elephant"), ruled the nation with her son. But Mbandzeni's widow Labotsibeni, though not of noble rank, was chosen for her intelligence, character, experience, and determination. Later, because of her tough dealings with the British and Boers, she would be called *Gwamile*, "The Indomitable." Bhunu, the adolescent son of Queen Labotsibeni, was named king.

For the annual ritual of kingship, the *Ncwala*, in 1899, priests were sent great distances to collect essential ingredients from the ocean, rivers, and forests. As the ritual reached its climax, tragedy struck: Bhunu collapsed and soon after was dead. Sobhuza, then only a few months old, was selected by the Council of Princes and his grandmother, Labotsibeni, who continued to rule, now as Queen Regent. In 1902, after the Anglo-Boer War, the British took control of Swaziland. Relations with whites became more tense when in 1907 a Land Partition Proclamation allotted two-thirds of the country to concessionaires, leaving only the remaining third for the entire Swazi population. Mbandzeni had granted concessions for 50 to 90 years, with 50-year renewals and right of reversal. Now title, upon expiration, could be converted at the wish of the leaseholder to private property under the British crown. The Swazi sent a delegation to England to petition Edward VII, as they would again send their most able spokesmen in the coming years to negotiate the freedom of the Swazi people.

When Sobhuza came of age, in 1921, the *Ncwala* was danced again for the first time in 21 years, investing him with the authority of kingship. The task for which Sobhuza was trained by his spirited grandmother would be to restore Swazi rights to the land and to their traditional way of life. Not that the Swazi would be a backward-facing people: they would have no choice, if they would survive, but to reckon with the Western ways now surrounding them. But they would try to do this with integrity, translating what was useful into a Swazi context and resisting those elements of European culture that would violate their essential being. The central feature of Swazi national identity was the institution of kingship and this they were not prepared to yield to the Western concept of a political democracy. Yet whites would be assured representation in the new Swazi government and Sobhuza's goal would be to defuse racial tensions and promote a degree of cooperation between blacks and whites rare among African polities. In 1967, when Sobhuza received the articles of government back from the British and was recognized by them as King, the British spoke of "granting independence." The Swazi spoke of *"regaining* independence," of regaining *inkulukho*, or freedom. As she indicates in the interview below, Hilda Kuper now wonders whether she has been correct to advocate so wholeheartedly Sobhuza's plan of government by kingship on the Swazi model when the King's immediate family, the Dlamini clan, is rapidly acquiring so much personal influence and power. It is one of the moral issues for her as a scholar looking at Swaziland in the broader historical context of the Third World and its conflicts of political ideologies, class, ethnicity, economics, and military alignments.

An Interview with Hilda Kuper, June 1979

In anthropology, nothing teaches like experience. In the following conversation, Hilda Kuper shares directly some of the experiences that were the backdrop to her biography of Sobhuza II, Ngwenyama and King of Swaziland. Naturally, these experiences are only part of a rich and complex relationship with the Swazi people. It is a relationship that has grown over the years and that continues to change: an anthropologist is perceived differently by particular individuals and groups as the historical scene shifts, and certain friendships are bound to develop more than others over time. This conversation offers a personal and spontaneous glimpse at the life-history enterprise as encountered by one anthropologist in one society. The fuller picture can be found in the biography, *Sobhuza II, Ngwenyama and King of Swaziland*, and in the other published works.

In writing the biography of Sobhuza II, Dr. Kuper, what were you trying to accomplish?

I used to say that the best of the rest of my life is going into this biography because it's so complicated to put a leader as a person in a broader historical setting, and this is what I was trying to do. I was trying to deal with Sobhuza the man, Sobhuza the King, and Swaziland, which had moved from a small, neglected British High

Commission Territory—it wasn't even a protectorate—to an independent kingdom recognized internationally. I wanted to make him understandable to non-Swazi but I also wanted Swazi generations to come to know that they had this particular leader.

People have the idea that somehow or other a polity just comes into being. It doesn't. There's discussion—what should we do in this case and that case? For instance, Sobhuza's way of choosing officials for new positions indicates the qualities he considers necessary for a person who will be taking important actions to have. Experience, knowledge, Western ways, Swazi ways. He plays the old and the young together. He says, "In a span of oxen, you need the old to pull the young, and the young must push the old." Or again, he wanted a name for a regiment, an age regiment started by Israelis for training in agriculture. He asked me. He asked lots of people. Takes notes. Writes down. Then he'll say, "Ah, that's good." Probably the name he's already had in mind, but he sifts round. In some ways, despite his pragmatism, he is too idealistic. Like in his search for an ideal constitution—one can't find an ideal constitution. It's one of those holy grails, difficult, if not impossible, to find.

But I think that one writes a biography largely because one's fascinated by the person. This is the first thing. I wouldn't have undertaken the biography of Sobhuza if I hadn't been interested in him as a person. And I also wanted to attempt an anthropological *tour de force*, in which the complexity of this particular historical situation could be brought out in terms of a central figure whom I knew.

Can you tell me how you came to undertake this commitment, which turned out to be a very difficult five-year task?

Well, I had this very warm relationship with the Swazi people because, as I said in the book, I came there in 1934. And I had lived there so long and gone there so frequently. And when Swaziland became independent, the new elected government decided that they should honor Sobhuza, because of the way he had led it to independence, by having somebody write his biography. I myself was reluctant at first. There were several people who wanted to do it, but it seemed to me that they all wanted it more for themselves in terms of career or reputation. And I think some of them would have done a better job than I did because they wouldn't have gone into the details. It would have been a more popular biography.

Meanwhile, a Swazi official phoned me again. I thought about it and finally took the initiative and wrote to the Prime Minister that if the government still wanted me to be the King's biographer, I would consider it a privilege. Then came a phone message from the late Msindazwe Sukati, who was then Swaziland's first Ambassador in the United States, and after congratulating me he said, "*Umuntfu obekiwe usheshe kufiwe.*" And I said, "Oh, my God, am I hearing you rightly?" And he translated it, literally, as, "A person who is appointed to a high position is in the process of being killed." Sukati happened to be quite well versed in Shakespeare and added, "In English you would say, 'Uneasy lies the head that wears a crown.'" You should not strive in traditional Swazi society for high positions because you're in danger of being killed. People who in the traditional society were closest to the king had to be prepared to lay down their lives for him, like the man mentioned in the book who went singing into the grave to accompany his royal master.

Did you know that you'd be working with a committee over your shoulder?
With a committee, yes. But I didn't realize that I would have to be so careful in my selection of material or have to maintain such a close tie with the committee. I only knew that the government would appoint people to help me. But this committee, appointed by the Cabinet and approved by the King, was more high powered than I might have expected. Acting as chair was the King's private secretary at the time, Mkhulunyelwa Matsebula, who is also a Swazi historian, responsible and discreet, and a writer of school textbooks and stories. Then there was Msindazwe Sukati, the man who phoned me—jovial, and shrewd, and diplomatic. He died shortly before the book came out. Then there was the Minister of Justice, Polycarp Dlamini, a cautious and troubled individual. I was pleased to have these people on the committee, because they all could contribute.

Despite my previous work, I had to do a good deal of additional research since the material required for the biography was different in quality and orientation from anything I had previously attempted. General anthropological concepts such as culture, function, structure, personality, roles, and process, were submerged, or perhaps converged. Though the focus was in some ways narrower, the perspective was broader and more historical. My task was to set the King, in his official role as well as in his uniqueness, within the context of his country, a small microcosm in a world of changes taking place at different levels and varying tempos. Sobhuza stated explicitly at one of our early meetings that this was not his autobiography, that I and the committee were responsible. My relationship with him changed—he became less approachable and I saw him less frequently and informally than in the past. He made it clear that he did not want to discuss the book—instead he asked me to put questions in writing and members of the committee had to be present at the interviews when he answered. Only sometimes was I allowed to tape his answers. This approach placed an additional limitation on the committee and I think this made the members excessively cautious in their scrutiny.

Together we agreed on how we could work together once I was back in America and writing. The problems were increased by distance. What happened was, when I had written a few chapters, I sent a copy to each member of the committee for comments. When the first chapters were returned I realized that there were certain things that were considered politically sensitive. The committee asked me to come to Swaziland for discussions and we read through and discussed every page of every chapter. Between 1972 and 1978, I made five visits to Swaziland for periods ranging from two weeks to several months and one visit to London for a special meeting with the publisher. I felt like a shuttlecock. I was going to and fro the whole time. It was interesting and something of a relief that once the book was published, Sobhuza and I returned to our earlier and more informal relationship.

The funding for the project came mainly from an individual grant to me by the Ford Foundation, and the Swazi contributed my housing while I was there.

You have said that you felt an obligation as an anthropologist to the Swazi people. What did this consist of?

My main obligation arose from gratitude and appreciation to the Swazi for the way they had let me into their lives. That is why I undertook this project in the first place. However, once I had begun the task and found it to be so difficult, my sense of professional and academic integrity was what led me to complete it. In 1934, I came a stranger, young, and ignorant, and the King and his family took me in and treated me with kindness and courtesy. When I was ill, I was looked after. One queen, laMatsebula, was sort of given to me as my mother, and I lived in the village of Sobhuza's mother, Lomawa. Sometimes friends would say, "We don't want you to publish this. These are *tinhlitiuo tethu*, our hearts, *tifihlo tethu*, our secrets. But we want *you* to know them because we want you to know *us*." And this is a very moving experience.

Initially they'd say about me, "*Nansi umlumbi*... there's a white person." After a while they began saying, "*Nansi umuntu* ... there is a person," using the word that they used for an African person, for one of themselves. Sometimes children would cry when I visited. This was in areas where they hadn't seen a white woman. And I once said to Sobhuza, "Oh, it's terrible, because one of the women threatened her child, 'That *umlumbi* is going to take you. She's a *sipokho* (a sort of bogey woman or spook) and is going to take you if you don't stop crying.' " And he said to me, "Wait a while. Soon that child will come to you and the mother will know you're one of us too."

I think that this degree of trust and confidence put me under a personal obligation and somehow justified my research. As an anthropologist who in some ways made my reputation from working in a foreign society, I feel too that I have an obligation to that *society* as well as to the individuals I came to know. In a review by David Brokinshaw in *African Arts*, he described Sobhuza as "one of the last of the great African kings," and that too is one of the reasons I felt his biography should be written.

Were you accepted equally by all the Swazi people or were you linked exclusively with the royal family? How did you feel about this?
It is hard to gauge "acceptance"—to distinguish actions from feelings. I won the confidence of a number of people, but by no means everyone. Some people probably loathed me because I was linked with the inner circle but were afraid to show hostility. All the time I felt myself accepted by some individuals, rejected by others. You can't be accepted by everyone, especially in a hierarchical society. You are always given an identity by others. *You* may want to identify with everybody, but there are cultural barriers—rank, age, sex, color, occupation. Thus it's usually difficult for a woman to get information from men, and for men to get information from women. I was

accepted or, rather, treated to some extent as a woman *and* as a man, in part because of the patronage of the Queen Mother, who held a major position in national affairs. I was given a conspicuous place in the hierarchy; sometimes I would be asked to stand with the queens, sometimes with the princesses. This is one of the reasons why I became so alerted to what I call "the African aristocracy." I was comfortable with this at that stage because then the ruling Swazi were fighting colonialism and racism. I have been told that at a pre-independence constitutional conference in London when different political factions put forward their views, one group referred to *An African Aristocracy*, while another group took with them my other book, *The Uniform of Colour*. They represented different perspectives of a political situation, originally written as part of a single work, published the same year, and their use by opposing parties would have been funny if the circumstances had not been so serious.

How did you handle the materials you received in confidence? Did you write them down and publish them eventually?

Confidence must be respected and the people protected. We've got to be very careful not to expose things that are given to us in confidence. I burnt my diaries. I was very ill one time when I came out of the field, terribly ill, and I thought I was going to die. At that stage I didn't know how private information could be handled. I should probably have put the diaries in a safe deposit box perhaps for 50 years. They were full of episodes which if I'd wanted to, I could have edited out, and so on. But I didn't write them for publication. I wrote them because of the way I was trained by Malinowski. I don't know if you know how he trained his students to have different notebooks. You have your diary, which you write up in the evening. You have your notebook, which you carry round. And you have another notebook where you draw up a map or anything visual. The diary is the personal side. It's how you are viewing other people. I think many of the anthropologists now would say that this is quite as important, this personal material. I turned some of it into a play, *A Witch in My Heart*, and some I wrote as fiction.

Do you feel that there is something remarkable about Sobhuza the man, himself, apart from his very special position as King?

I think there's something definitely remarkable about him. The structure of kingship is there, was there, but it could have been shifted had he been weaker and more prepared to compromise principles. There is now a great deal of tension because Swaziland is between the Republic of South Africa—with its policy of apartheid—and the Marxist-oriented regime of Samora Machel in Mozambique. What has happened to African kings elsewhere may happen in Swaziland. Everyone is aware of that. But the meeting between Samora Machel and Sobhuza, which I describe in the biography, is a dramatic example of Sobhuza's ability to balance the tightrope. The meeting was at Sobhuza's request, arranged by Msindazwe Sukati, who was then Swaziland's first ambassador in Mozambique. Machel came with armed soldiers in military lorries. Sukati told me that many Swazi councilors were terrified when they heard, and asked, "Is this a visit or is it an invasion?" But Sobhuza said, "It will be all right." He went to meet him wearing his usual, informal traditional clothing—his *mahia*, the native shirt, and barefoot. They had a wonderful talk. Most disarming man, he is. The relationship is much better between those two countries than one would anticipate.

Economically, Swaziland has South Africa as the strong man, yet politically and ideologically Swaziland has made a very real stand against apartheid. But Swaziland is confronted with all the problems of modernization, and in the popular press Swaziland has been described as "the Las Vegas of South Africa," and Sobhuza as "a black king of a South African playground." He is outraged at these distortions. It is the whole question of whether tourism is a good thing or a bad thing. The argument is that hotels and casinos bring in money and employment. But Sobhuza is aware and critical of the social costs—prostitution and the humiliation and exploitation of the Swazi by whites from South Africa who are accustomed to treat blacks as servants and inferiors. Because he is not a dictator, or a racist, Sobhuza follows the advice of advisors who I sometimes think are not good advisors.

One of the ways in which Sobhuza is trying to meet the challenges is through education of his people. His primary interest is in education for social, practical purposes. He is committed to developing the technical expertise of his people so that they can occupy the top positions in industry and commerce. But his main aim is the best development of the land—agriculture, cattle keeping, forestry, so that the countryside does not become desolated. It is his greatest urge to

keep the people happy on the land and not to create a semi-educated,
unemployed urban population. There is also his own interest in
education as opening up exciting fields of knowledge. He's extremely
interested in the customs of other people. He'll ask the most
unexpected question about the most remote people whom he's
suddenly heard of. He'll say, "How do they dress? What do they eat?
How do they marry?" He is very adroit at dealing with people with
humor and diplomacy, sometimes using anecdotes and putting
questions as a diversion. Sometimes he uses this when the conversation with a political figure becomes a bit difficult for him. When he
doesn't want to commit himself, he will introduce extraordinary
anthropological facts! He didn't have anthing like the education of
many of the ordinary people in Westernized countries. But he had a
tremendously intelligent South African coloured man, Grandon, as
his first teacher. I knew Grandon, and Grandon always used to say to
him, "Think. Always think." And he thinks. He says now, "I don't
speak rashly," and he doesn't. He is careful in what he says. His is
indeed a difficult role which he has played with consummate skill.
But now that he is becoming quite old and the situation more critical,
his position may require flexibility and knowledge beyond his ability.

*You have known Sobhuza as a political figure and as a private individual.
Does he always play the monarch or is there a personal side too?*
There is definitely an important private side. As I explain in the
book, the Swazi say "The King is a king twice. He is king of his family
and king of the nation." I tried to play down the personal side in the
section on the wives, the queens, and at the same time to indicate that
he was a private person and had a rich private life. But it was more on
Ngwenyama, King of the Swazi, that I had to focus. When we left, the
last thing he said was, "Look, look. I've just got a photograph of this
little one." He loves children and he'd just received a big color
photograph of one of his favorites. The children are adorable. And I
couldn't . . . I didn't want to . . . I just didn't want to deal with that
side of him. And yet I brought out quite a lot of it—his relationship
to his mother and his sister, and that very moving scene with his
"son," whom we would call his nephew, the political rebel who had
been imprisoned. It is very hard to separate the personal from the
political in a society structured by kinship.

Sobhuza is portrayed as the leader of a government that is enlightened, responsible, and stable. Is this only the official version?

This is an official biography and represents the image that the government wished to portray, but all the time I tried to give the criticisms that Sobhuza was meeting and the way in which he replied to those criticisms. Now there are certain things which I fear are impinging on that ideal kingdom. I only hinted at them in the book. There is increasing "Dlaminization," a granting of too much power to the immediate family. One of the things they would not let me put into the book was the complete genealogy of the queens, their children, and their parentage, because that is politically sensitive— too sensitive since Sobhuza's heir is not yet known publicly. The decision will be made in terms of complex principles of succession. A king is not only a king by his father but by his mother. His mother is chosen from among all other queens in the harem by such factors as the clan of her parents, her relationship to past kings, and finally her character. From the way in which I presented my genealogy, one might predict the most likely contestants. The genealogy is locked up in the archives in Swaziland. The choice will be left to the Council of Princes.

The British, by recognizing Sobhuza as Paramount Chief from the Dlamini clan, gave that clan its present security. Some people say that had Sobhuza retained the Western constitution introduced by the British, a constitutional monarchy would have been assured in Swaziland. In the past, all factions respected Sobhuza personally. But now some of the more radical say that there's an autocracy. In theory, modern Western society is not ascriptive but is competitive and individualistic. But in the traditional African kingdom, hereditary privilege is accepted and the king is obligated to his kinsmen. The clan itself is a corporate unit. The Dlaminization is disturbing, and there *is* evidence of corruption, yet I also feel that the structure has become so well developed that it does make for stability. If a non-Dlamini tries to get the position of king, it may have devastating repercussions on the ordinary people. Sobhuza himself was concerned with the interests of all his subjects. He used to say very often, and this is an old and widespread African axiom: *"Nkosi inkosi ngebantu . . .* a ruler is ruler by his people," and unless he has the support of his people, he is helpless. And another axiom is, "A ruler is ruler by his councilors, his *tindvuna*." Among the Swazi, the councilors are always non-Dlamini. So there are checks and balances on Dlaminization. The battle of independence for the people was carried by Sobhuza, and he very often bore the brunt of political antagonism.

Were you personally criticized for what you wrote in the book?

As I said before, one of the things I wanted to do was to bring out the complexity of the historical situation. There was one case I talk about in which a Swazi who claimed to have been born in Swaziland was elected to Parliament and then was rejected because it was proved he wasn't born in Swaziland and therefore was ineligible for election. The matter was indeed badly handled and I was criticized very much for defending in any way the government's action. But more aliens are coming in than the Swazi can cope with. Some, particularly from South Africa, are refugees hostile to the government, and it *is* in a vulnerable position. My critics stated that if I were in South Africa, I would express a different point of view on various issues, but the South African government is not the Swazi government. Perhaps I could have been more critical. Perhaps I should have been.

What was Sobhuza's own reaction to your biography of him?

It was interesting that he said to me, "This book, I don't want to read this book. You've got to say what you're going to say." When I was there in 1978 to present him with his copy, he asked, "Now, what have you said about the land? What have you said about it?" Before he would see me ... this was very interesting ... when Leo and I came down, Sobhuza had a message waiting for me at the hotel. "Phone Matsebula." And he said, "Ngwenyama's just called and asked, 'What does laBima say in this book about the land and the concessionaires and the way in which my grandfather, Mbandzeni said, '*I did not sell the land*'?" So I had to look it up and I found three references. Matsebula then took these to him. He read them through. Then it was finally, "Bring her. Bring them in." You see, it was a matter of national importance, which he wanted to be set straight.

Now that the book is finished, do you feel that you have managed to portray the truth about the subject of this biography?

The question of the truth of biography is one that interests me very much. As an anthropologist, I have tried to show that the biography of a man such as Sobhuza involves not only a knowledge of a foreign society but a different approach to the individual, including the self. We find in Swaziland a king who built a modern nation within a political system in which leadership was not sought after, in which rivalry was considered destructive, in which consultation at different levels was essential, and in which national interests were considered more important than the freedom of the king himself. Power and privilege are inherent in the kingship; but for Sobhuza, his inherited position spelled responsibility, self-restraint, respect for others, and also the courage to express unpopular opinions for unselfish reasons. To my mind, he has filled his position with humility and dignity, and stands out in modern history as a good King, a wise statesman, a gracious man. Other interpretations tend to be more critical and sometimes hostile. My information showed that Sobhuza never acted on legal advice without the support of his councils. Jack Halpern, a well known journalist whose book *South African Hostages* is widely read and often quoted, interprets the phrase, "The Mouth That Speaks No Lies" as the approach of an autocrat whose words may not be challenged; Sobhuza's supporters explain it as his obligation to express a general consensus, or, in his own words, "I am my people's mouthpiece."

What is the truth, or, more exactly, where does truth lie? It appears that there is no single truth, nor even different angles and perceptions of truth, but several possible truths according to individual experience and commitment. A biography is not a case of six characters in search of an author, but of six authors in search of a character, and when they find him they might not recognize him, and in any case each will see him differently. Awareness of the complexity of the human being leads to an acknowledgement that we can never know the absolute truth of experience. We *can* look at different statements about how our subject constructed reality at different times in his life, yet even his own self-perceptions are changing and selective. But my final point is that biographies are not written in a vacuum. They reflect different levels of reality. At one level they are reflections of the self in complex interaction with others; at another level they are empirical data affecting real people. In the case of political figures the second level is the more significant, revealing conflicting political currents with implications for future action in a world of events beyond the self, and far more powerful.

Toward a Theory of Personal Action in Contemporary Culture

If there is one point that we might wish to emphasize in this chapter, it is that through the work of writing about lives—our own, and the lives of others—we can humanize ourselves. The acts of empathy that arise in attempting to understand the reality of people sometimes very different from ourselves can be a transformative process. Such acts of empathy, whether successful or not in actually simulating the other person's experience, help us to break down the barriers of ego and identity that give us each the illusion of somehow standing separate and apart from the flow of human consciousness through the millenia. Such an empathic perspective on the world today may be of benefit in the face of narrowly defined sectarian interests.

Many of the key institutions of Western culture, from the democratic state to the nuclear family, are under siege. Some say they should properly give way to new social structures, while others will argue that our survival depends upon them. Whatever one's position in this debate, it is necessary to have some underlying theory linking the self to society, since our personal actions have much to do with the form our future society takes. Traditionally, the task of the life history in anthropology has been to link "culture" with "personality," and "society" with the "self." Certain critics, among them historian Christopher Lasch (1978), trace the current inadequacies of Western institutions to the emphasis since the mid-nineteenth century on competitive individualism. Describing what he calls "the new narcissism," Lasch attacks the shallow and hedonistic sense of self encouraged by a commercialism that markets sex itself in advertising and pornography and that promotes consumption as a way of life. The resulting values hold that celebrity is more important than achievement, while the present obscures the future and the past, sexual freedoms fail to offer emotional satisfaction, tenuous intimacies deflect action from wider political commitment, and old age brings only dread of death.

For anthropologist Barbara Myerhoff (personal communication), the life history is a research tool that holds within it tremendous power for developing the human potential of those who use it. The method teaches a focusing on small things, in which the small becomes laden with significance and points beyond itself. It has to do with noticing details one never saw before, framing them, ordering them and giving them names. The enterprise of keeping a journal or of recording someone else's life does this. And it provides the rub necessary to articulate one's own self against the background of previously unperceived alternatives. This intensification of perception becomes the symbolic life, coordinating inner and outer existence. To Myerhoff, it is also the moral life:

> I think "unimportant people" have a greater chance of finding this out. It goes back to the oral tradition. Nothing elite, formal, and learned can get in the way of it. Women very often are the ones who have this understanding as outsiders, as you can see in the last chapter of *Number Our Days*. Of course, liminal people of all sorts have it. Women, prisoners, travelers, the dispossessed, very often have reached it, and other great keepers of journals. We know it is a learning tool. We know it is therapeutic. We know it is profoundly validating. We know it makes for human connections. It is *also*, and perhaps only for this society and not for others, a phase or piece of work in moral development.

Asked how she came to understand these things and find them true, Myerhoff credits two of her teachers: "I've had two teachers I completely trust," she explains. "One is Hilda Kuper, with whom I studied anthropology at UCLA. And one was Shmuel, who appears in *Number Our Days*. It is so clear that teachers like this want your growth and that they are forcing you to question. It's a forcing, a forcing of patience, a reflectiveness, a kind of listening, a continual selection. It forces such a complex relationship to them and what they are saying that it goes far beyond the usual kind of teaching, the teaching that merely asserts how things are. You can never be the same after that," she concludes, "because it forces you to pay attention to people in a different way. That's the humanization: You can never dismiss people again, and although you may not have the time to live that way, or the energy, or the spirit, or the appetite for it, once you do it, even if once, it is a transformative experience."

References

The authors note with pleasure the growth of important work in the life-history field. We regret, however, that as a consequence a comprehensive bibliography can no longer be encompassed within a general review such as this.

Aberle, David F.
1951
"The Psychosocial Analysis of a Hopi Life-History." *Comparative Psychology Monographs*, vol. 21, no. 1.

Abraham, Karl
1955
"Amenhotep IV: A Psycho-Analytical Contribution towards the Understanding of His Personality and of the Monotheistic Cult of Aton." In *Clinical Papers and Essays on Psycho-Analysis*. London: Hogarth. Pp. 262–290. (Originally published in 1912.)

Adams, Henry
1918
The Education of Henry Adams: An Autobiography. Boston: Houghton Mifflin. (Numerous reprints.)

Adler, Alfred
1929
Problems of Neurosis: A Book of Case-Histories. London: Kegan Paul. New York: Harper (1964).

Agar, Michael H.
1980
The Professional Stranger: An Informal Introduction to Ethnography. New York: Academic Press.

Allport, Gordon
1942
The Use of Personal Documents in Psychological Science. New York: Social Science Research Council, Bulletin 49.

American Anthropological Association
1973
Professional Ethics: Statements and Procedures. Washington, D.C.: The Association.

Anderson, Eva Greenslit
1943
Chief Seattle. Caldwell, Idaho: Caxton.

Anderson, Rufus
1825
Memoir of Catherine Brown, A Christian Indian of the Cherokee Nation. Boston: Crocker & Brewster (2nd edition).

Angell, Robert
1945
"A Critical Review of the Development of the Personal Document Method in Sociology 1910–1940." In Louis Gottschalk et al., 1945. Pp. 177–233.

Anonymous (Samuel G. Goodrich)
1843
Lives of Celebrated American Indians. Boston: Bradbury, Soden & Co.

Anonymous
1872
Memoir of the Distinguished Mohawk Indian Chief, Sachem and Warrior, Captain Joseph Brant. Brantford, Ontario: C.E. Stewart & Co.

Apes, William
1831
A Son of the Forest, the Experience of William Apes, A Native of the Forest. Written by Himself. New York: G.F. Bumce (2nd edition).

Augustine
1961
The Confessions of Saint Augustine. Edward B. Pusey, trans. New York: Collier Books. (Written 397 A.D.)

Austin, Mary H.
1915
The Arrow-Maker: A Drama in Three Acts. Boston and New York: Houghton Mifflin.

Baldwin, James
1955
Notes of a Native Son. Boston: Beacon Press. (Original 1949.)

Bandelier, Adolph F.A.
1890
The Delight Makers. New York: Dodd, Mead.

Barbeau, Charles Marius
1928
The Downfall of Temlaham. Toronto: Macmillan.

Barnes, J.A.
1967
"Some Ethical Problems in Modern Field Work." In D.G. Jongmans and P.C.W. Gutkind, eds., *Anthropologists in the Field.* New York: Humanities Press. Pp. 193–213.

1979
Who Should Know What? Social Science, Privacy, and Ethics. Cambridge: Cambridge University Press.

Barnett, Louise K.
1975
The Ignoble Savage: American Literary Racism 1790–1890. Westport, Connecticut: Greenwood Press.

Barrett, S.M.
1906
Geronimo's Story of His Life. New York: Duffield & Co.

Bartlett, Frederic Charles
1967
Remembering: A Study in Experimental and Social Psychology. Cambridge: Cambridge University Press. (Original 1932.)

Barton, Roy F.
1963
Autobiographies of Three Pagans in the Philippines. New Hyde Park, N.Y.: University Books. (First published in England in 1938.)

Basso, Keith H.
1979
Portraits of "The Whiteman": Linguistic Play and Cultural Symbols among the Western Apache. Cambridge: Cambridge University Press.

Bateson, Gregory (Ed.)
1974
Perceval's Narrative: A Patient's Account of His Psychosis, 1830–1832. New York: William Morrow.

Bateson, Gregory, and Margaret Mead
1942
Balinese Character: A Photographic Analysis. Special publications of the New York Academy of Sciences, 2. New York: The Academy.

Beal, Merrill D.
1963
"I Will Fight No More Forever": Chief Joseph and the Nez Perce War. Seattle: University of Washington Press.

Beals, Frank L.
1943
Chief Black Hawk. Chicago: Wheeler Publishing Co.

Beals, Ralph
1953
"Acculturation." In A.L. Kroeber, ed., 1953. Pp. 621–641.

Becker, Howard S.
1970
"Problems of Inference and Proof in Participant Observation." In William J. Filstead, ed., 1970. Pp. 189–201.

Becker, Howard S., and Anselm L. Strauss
1956
"Careers, Personality, and Adult Socialization." *American Journal of Sociology* 62:253–263.

Berreman, Gerald
1968
"Is Anthropology Alive? Social Responsibility in Social Anthropology." *Current Anthropology* 9(5):391–396.

Bidney, David (Ed.)
1963
The Concept of Freedom in Anthropology. (Studies in General Anthropology, I.) The Hague: Mouton & Co.

Binswanger, Ludwig
1960
"The Existential Analysis School of Thought." In R. May, E. Angel, and H. Ellenberger, eds., *Existence: A New Dimension in Psychiatry and Psychology*. New York: Basic Books. Pp. 191–213.

1963
Being in the World: Selected Papers. Jacob Needleman, trans. New York: Basic Books.

Biocca, Ettore
1971
Yanoáma: The Narrative of a White Girl Kidnapped by Amazonian Indians. New York: Dutton.

Black Hawk
1834
Life of Ma-Ka-Tai-Me-She-Kia-Kiak or Black Hawk. Dictated by himself. Boston: Russell, Odiorne & Metcalf.

Blacking, John
1964
Black Background: The Childhood of a South African Girl. New York: Abelard-Schuman.

Blasing, Mutlu K.
1977
The Art of Life: Studies in American Autobiographical Literature. Austin: University of Texas Press.

Blumer, George
1949
"History Taking." New Haven: Yale Medical Library. Reprinted from *Connecticut State Medical Journal*, vol. 13.

Blumer, H.
1939
"An Appraisal of Thomas and Znaniecki's *The Polish Peasant in Europe and America*." Critiques of Research in the Social Sciences, 1. New York: Social Science Research Council, Bulletin 44.

Bogdan, Robert
1974
Being Different: The Autobiography of Jane Fry. New York: Wiley.

1977
"Voices: First Person Life Histories as a Method of Studying Retardates." Paper Presented at the 101st Annual Convention of the American Association of Mental Retardation. New Orleans, June, 1977.

Bogdan, Robert, and S.J. Taylor
1975
Introduction to Qualitative Research Methods: A Phenomenological Approach to the Social Sciences. New York: Wiley.

1976
"The Judged, Not the Judge: An Insider's View of Mental Retardation." *American Psychologist* 31(1):47–52.

Borden, Philip
1970
"Found Cumbering the Soil. Manifest Destiny and the Indian in the Nineteenth Century." In Gary B. Nash and Richard Weiss, eds., *The Great Fear.* New York: Holt. Pp. 71–97.

Borges, Jorge Luis
1962
"Funes the Memorious." In *Ficciones.* New York: Grove Press. Pp. 107–117.

Bornet, Vaughn Davis
1955
"Oral History *Can* Be Worthwhile." *American Archivist* 18:241–253.

Boss, Medard
1963
Psychoanalysis and Daseinanalysis. Ludwig B. Lefebre, trans. New York: Basic Books. (Original 1957.)

Boswell, James
1904
The Life of Samuel Johnson, LL.D. London: Oxford University Press. (Original 1791.)

Bott, Elizabeth
1957
Family and Social Network: Roles, Norms and External Relationships in Ordinary Urban Families. London: Tavistock.

Bowen, Elenore Smith
1954
Return to Laughter. New York: Harper. London: Gollancz.

Brant, Charles S. (Ed.)
1969
Jim Whitewolf: The Life of a Kiowa Apache Indian. New York: Dover.

Briggs, Jean L.
1970
Never in Anger: Portrait of an Eskimo Family. Cambridge, Mass.: Harvard University Press.

Brim, Orville G.
1968
"Adult Socialization." In John Clausen, ed., *Socialization and Society.* Boston: Little, Brown.

Brim, Orville G., and Stanton Wheeler
1966
Socialization after Childhood: Two Essays. New York: Wiley.

Britt, Albert
1938
Great Indian Chiefs. New York: McGraw-Hill.

Brown, Claude
1965
Manchild in the Promised Land. New York: Macmillan.

Brown, Dee Alexander
1971
Bury My Heart at Wounded Knee. New York: Holt.

Bruss, Elizabeth W.
1976
Autobiographical Acts: The Changing Situation of a Literary Genre. Baltimore: Johns Hopkins University Press.

Bruyn, Severyn T.
1970a
"The Methodology of Participant Observation." In William J. Filstead, ed., 1970. Pp. 305–327.

1970b
"The New Empiricists: The Participant Observer and Phenomenologist." In William J. Filstead, ed., 1970. Pp. 283–287.

Bühler, Charlotte
1933
Der Menschliche Lebenslauf als Psychologisches Problem. Leipzig: S. Hirzel Verlag.

1935
"The Curve of Life as Studied in Biographies." *Journal of Applied Psychology* 19:405–409.

1961
"Meaningful Living in the Mature Years." In R. Kleemeier, ed., *Aging and Leisure.* New York: Oxford University Press.

Bühler, Charlotte, and Fred Massarik (Eds.)
1968
The Course of Human Life: A Study of Goals in the Humanistic Perspective. New York: Springer.

Burton, Arthur, and Robert E. Harris (Eds.)
1955
Clinical Studies of Personality. New York: Harper.

Butler, Robert N.
1968
"The Life Review: An Interpretation of Reminiscences in the Aged." In Bernice L. Neugarten, ed., *Middle Age and Aging: A Reader in Social Psychology.* Chicago: University of Chicago Press. Pp. 486–496.

Cain, Leonard D., Jr.
1964
"Life Course and Social Structure." In Robert E.L. Faris, ed., *Handbook of Modern Sociology.* Chicago: Rand McNally. Pp. 272–309.

Cameron, Norman
1963
Personality Development and Psychopathology: A Dynamic Approach. Boston: Houghton Mifflin.

Cannell, C.F., and R.L. Kahn
1953
"The Collection of Data by Interviewing." In L. Festinger and D. Katz, eds., *Research Methods in the Behavioral Sciences.* New York: Dryden Press. Pp. 327–380.

Carstairs, G. Morris
1958
The Twice-Born: A Study of a Community of High-Caste Hindus. Bloomington: Indiana University Press.

Cartwright, Dorwin, and John R.P. French, Jr.
1939
"The Reliability of Life-History Studies." *Character and Personality* 8:110–119.

Cassell, Joan
1977
A Group Called Women: Sisterhood and Symbolism in the Feminist Movement. New York: McKay.

1978
"Risk and Benefit to Subjects of Fieldwork." *American Sociologist* 13(August):134–143.

Caughey, John L.
1979
"Introspection in the Ethnography of Consciousness." Paper presented in a session on "The Reflexive Anthropologist: Rethinking Our Concepts and Approaches," at the 78th Annual Meeting of the American Anthropological Association, Cincinnati, Ohio. November 30, 1979.

Chagnon, Napoleon A.
1968
Yąnomamö: The Fierce People. New York: Holt.

1974
Studying the Yąnomamö. New York: Holt.

Chalmers, Harvey
1955
Joseph Brant: Mohawk. East Lansing, Michigan: Michigan State University Press.

1962
The Last Stand of the Nez Perce: Destruction of a People. New York: Twayne Publishers.

Chapin, Howard M.
1931
Sachems of the Narragansetts. Providence: Rhode Island Historical Society.

Chilungu, Simeon W.
1976
"Issues in the Ethics of Research Method: An Interpretation of the Anglo-American Perspective." *Current Anthropology* 17(3):457–482.

Christians, Clifford G.
1977
"Fifty Years of Scholarship in Media Ethics." *Journal of Communication* 27(4):19–29.

Clifford, James L. (Ed.)
1962
Biography as an Art. New York: Oxford University Press.

Collier, John
1967
Visual Anthropology: Photography as a Research Method. New York: Holt.

Collins, Glenn
1980
"Men's and Women's Speech: How They Differ." *New York Times,* Style Section C18–19. November 17.

Colvard, Richard
1967
"Interaction and Identification in Reporting Field Research: A Critical Reconsideration of Protective Procedures." In Gideon Sjoberg, ed., *Ethics, Politics, and Social Research.* Cambridge, Mass.: Schenkman. Pp. 319–358.

Cooley, Thomas
1976
Educated Lives: The Rise of Modern Autobiography in America. Columbus: Ohio State University Press.

Copway, George
1847
The Life, History, and Travels of Kah-Ge-Ga-Gah-Bowh (George Copway), A Young Indian Chief of the Ojibwa Nation. Written by himself. Philadelphia: James Harmstead. (6th edition.)

Cornelisen, Ann
1976
Women of the Shadows. Boston: Little, Brown and Atlantic Monthly Press.

Cox, James M.
1971
"Autobiography and America." In J.H. Miller, ed. *Aspects of Narrative.* New York: Columbia University Press. Pp. 252–277.

Crapanzano, Vincent
1969
The Fifth World of Enoch Maloney: Portrait of a Navaho. New York: Random House.

1972
The Fifth World of Forster Bennett: Portrait of a Navaho. New York: Viking Press.

1977a
"On the Writing of Ethnography." *Dialectical Anthropology* II:69–73.

1977b
"The Life History in Anthropological Field Work." *Anthropology and Humanism Quarterly* 2(2–3):3-7.

1980
Tuhami: Portrait of a Moroccan. Chicago: University of Chicago Press.

Crapanzano, Vincent, and Vivian Garrison (Eds.)
1977
Case Studies in Spirit Possession. New York: Wiley.

Croce, Benedetto
1959
"History and Chronicle." In Hans Meyerhoff, ed., *The Philosophy of History in Our Time.* Garden City, N.Y.: Doubleday. Pp. 44–57.

Cuffe, Paul
1839
Narrative of the Life and Adventures of Paul Cuffe, A Pequot Indian: During Thirty Years Spent at Sea and in Travelling in Foreign Lands. Vernon, Conn.: H.N. Bill.

Cumming, Elaine, and W.E. Henry
1961
Growing Old: The Process of Disengagement. New York: Basic Books.

Dailey, Charles A.
1971
Assessment of Lives: Personality Evaluation in a Bureacratic Society. San Francisco: Jossey-Bass.

Daly, Mary
1973
Beyond God the Father: Toward a Philosophy of Women's Liberation. Boston: Beacon Press.

1975
The Church and the Second Sex: With a New Feminist Postchristian Introduction by the Author. New York: Harper.

1978
Gyn/Ecology: The Metaethics of Radical Feminism. Boston: Beacon Press.

Davis, Allison, and John Dollard
1940
Children of Bondage. New York: Harper.

Davis, Shelton H.
1977
Victims of the Miracle: Development and the Indians of Brazil. Cambridge, England: Cambridge University Press.

de Beauvoir, Simone
1952
The Second Sex. New York: Vintage Books.

DeJesus, Carolina Maria
1962
Child of the Dark: The Diary of Carolina Maria DeJesus. New York: New American Library.

Deloria, Vine, Jr.
1970
Custer Died for Your Sins. New York: Avon Books.

Deutscher, I.
1962
"Socialization for Post-Parental Life." In Arnold M. Rose, ed., *Human Behavior and Social Processes.* Boston: Houghton Mifflin. Pp. 506–525.

Devereux, George
1967
From Anxiety to Method in the Behavioral Sciences. The Hague: Mouton & Co.

Diener, Edward, and Rick Crandall
1978
Ethics in Social and Behavioral Research. Chicago: University of Chicago Press.

Dohrenwend, Barbara Snell, and S.A. Richardson
1963
"Directiveness and Non-directiveness in Research Interviewing: A Reformulation of the Problem." *Psychological Bulletin* 60:475–485.

Dollard, John
1935
Criteria for the Life History (with analysis of six notable documents). New Haven: Yale University Press.

Drake, Benjamin
1841
Life of Tecumseh, and of His Brother the Prophet; With a Historical Sketch of the Shawanoe Indian. Cincinnati: E. Morgan & Co.

1854
The Great Indian Chief of the West: or, Life and Adventures of Black Hawk. Cincinnati: Applegate & Co.

Drake, Samuel
1880
The Aboriginal Races of North America. New York: Hurst.

DuBois, Cora A.
1937
"Some Psychological Objectives and Techniques in Ethnography." *Journal of Social Psychology* 8:285–301.

1944
The People of Alor. Minneapolis: University of Minnesota Press.

1960
"Two Decades Later." In *The People of Alor.* New York: Harper. Pp. xvi-xxx.

Dumont, Jean-Paul
1978
The Headman and I. Austin: University of Texas Press.

Dyk, Walter
1938
Son of Old Man Hat: A Navaho Autobiography Recorded by Walter Dyk. With an introduction by Edward Sapir. New York: Harcourt.

Earle, William
1972
The Autobiographical Consciousness: A Philosophical Inquiry into Existence. Chicago: Quadrangle Books.

Eastman, Charles A.
1902
Indian Boyhood. New York: McClure.

Edel, Leon
1959
Literary Biography. New York: Doubleday.

Edgerton, Robert B.
1964
"Pokot Intersexuality: An East African Example of the Resolution of Sexual Incongruity." *American Anthropologist* 66(6)(Part 2):1288–1299.

1965
"Some Dimensions of Disillusionment in Culture Contact." *Southwestern Journal of Anthropology* 21(3)(Autumn):231–243.

1967
The Cloak of Competence: Stigma in the Lives of the Mentally Retarded. Berkeley: University of California Press.

1976
Deviance: A Cross-Cultural Perspective. Menlo Park, California: Cummings.

1978
(Principal Investigator). "The Community Context of Normalization." NICHD Grant No. 09424–02.

Edgerton, Robert B., and L.L. Langness
1978
"Observing Mentally Retarded Persons in Community Settings: An Anthropological Perspective." In Gene P. Sackett, ed., *Observing Behavior Volume I: Theory and Applications in Mental Retardation*, Baltimore: University Park Press. Pp. 335–348.

Eggleston, Edward, and L.E. Seelye
1878
Tecumseh and the Shawnee Prophet. New York: Dodd, Mead.

1879
Brant and Red Jacket. New York: Dodd, Mead.

Ekvall, Robert B.
1960
Faithful Echo. New Haven: College and University Press.

Elkin, A.P.
1941
"Native Languages and the Field Worker in Australia." *American Anthropologist.* 43:89–94.

Ellis, Edward S.
1861
The Life of Pontiac, the Conspirator, Chief of the Ottawas. New York: Beadle & Co.

Elmendorf, Mary Lindsay
1976
Nine Mayan Women: A Village Faces Change. Cambridge, Mass.: Schenkman.

Enimikeeso
1867
The Indian Chief: An Account of the Labours, Losses, Sufferings, and Oppression of Ke-Zig-Koe-E. Ne-Ne (David Sawyer) a Chief of the Ojibeway Indians in Canada West. London: William Nichols.

Erikson, Erik H.
1958
Young Man Luther: A Study in Psychoanalysis and History. New York: Norton.

1968
"Life Cycle." In *International Encyclopedia of the Social Sciences,* vol. 9, 286–92.

1969
Gandhi's Truth: On the Origins of Militant Nonviolence. New York: Norton.

1975
Life History and the Historical Moment. New York: Norton.

Evans-Pritchard, E.E.
1940
The Nuer. Oxford: Clarendon Press.

Fabian, Johannes
1971
"On Professional Ethics and Epistemological Foundations." *Current Anthropology* 12(2):230–232.

Fee, Chester A.
1936
Chief Joseph: The Biography of a Great Indian. New York: Wilson-Erickson.

Filstead, William J. (Ed.)
1970
Qualitative Methodology. Chicago: Markham.

Fivars, G. (Ed.)
1973
The Critical Incident Technique: A Bibliography. Palo Alto: American Institute for Research.

Flanagan, J.C.
1954
"The Critical Incident Technique." *Psychology Bulletin* 51:327–358.

Ford, Clellan S.
1941
Smoke from Their Fires. New Haven: Yale Univesity Press.

Foreman, Grant
1938
Sequoyah. Norman: University of Oklahoma Press.

Foster, George E.
1885
Se-Quo-Yah. The American Cadmus and Modern Moses. A Complete Biography of the Greatest of Redmen. Philadelphia: Office of the Indian Rights Association.

Frank, Gelya
1975
The Petitions of 1911: An Ethnohistorical Account of Economic Factionalism on the Tule River Indian Reservation. M.A. thesis, Department of Anthropology, University of California, Los Angeles.

1979a
"Finding the Common Denominator: A Phenomenological Critique of Life History Method." *Ethos 7(1)(Spring):68–94.*

1979b
"Venus on Wheels: Self-Image and Collective Myth in the Life History of a Congenital Amputee." Paper presented at the annual meeting of the American Folklore Association, Los Angeles, October 25.

1980a
"Life Histories in Gerontology: The Subjective Side to Aging." In Christine L. Fry and Jennie Keith, eds., *New Methods for Old Age Research: Anthropological Alternatives*. Chicago: Center for the Study of Urban Policy, Loyola University. Distributed by the Association for Anthropology and Gerontology. (Pp. 155–176.)

1980b
"History of Land Tenure for the Tule River Indian Tribe." In *Restoration of Tule River Indian Reservation Lands,* pp. 74–141. (Hearing Before the United States

Senate Select Committee on Indian Affairs, 96th Congress, 1st Session. On S. 1998 to Provide for the United States to Hold in Trust for the Tule River Indian Tribe Certain Public Domain Lands Formerly Removed from the Tule River Indian Reservation. February 5, 1980.) Washington, D.C.: U.S. Government Printing Office.

1980c
"Intervention: Ethics and Objectivity in Participant Observation with the Mildly Retarded." Working Paper No. 17 of the Socio-Behavioral Group, Mental Retardation Research Center, School of Medicine, University of California, Los Angeles.

1981
Venus on Wheels: The Life History of a Congenital Amputee. Doctoral Dissertation. Department of Anthropology, University of California, Los Angeles.

In press
"Mercy's Children." *The Anthropology and Humanism Quarterly.* (Ethnographic fiction, with a preface by the author.)

Frankl, Viktor E.
1963
Man's Search for Meaning: An Introduction to Logotherapy. Preface by Gordon Allport. New York: Washington Square Press.

Franklin, Benjamin
1949
Memoirs. Parallel Text Edition. Berkeley: University of California Press.

Freeman, James M.
1979
Untouchable: An Indian Life History. Stanford: Stanford University Press.

French, Marilyn
1977
The Women's Room. New York: Jove Publications, Inc.

Frenkel, Else
1936
"Studies in Biographic Psychology." *Character and Personality* 5:1–34.

Freud, Sigmund
1909
"Analysis of a Phobia in a Five-Year-Old Boy." *Standard Edition of the Complete Psychological Works.* James Strachey, trans. London: Hogarth Press, 1958. Vol. 10, pp. 5–149.

1910
Leonardo da Vinci, A Study in Psychosexuality. A.A. Brill, trans. New York: Random House, 1947.

1911
"Psycho-Analytic Notes on an Autobiographical Account of a Case of Paranoia." *Standard Edition of the Complete Psychological Works*. James Strachey, trans. London: Hogarth Press, 1958. Vol. 12, pp. 9–82.

Garfinkel, Harold
1967
"Passing and the Managed Achievement of Sex Status in an 'Intersexed' Person: Part 1." In *Studies in Ethnomethodology*, Englewood Cliffs, N.J.: Prentice-Hall. Pp. 116–185.

Garnett, David
1933
Pocahontas; or, the Nonparell of Virginia. New York: Harcourt.

Garst, Shannon
1953
Chief Joseph of the Nez Perce. New York: Messner.

Gass, W.H.
1970
Fiction and the Figures of Life. New York: Knopf.

Geertz, Clifford
1973
The Interpretation of Cultures. New York: Basic Books. Pp. 3–30 ("Thick Description: Toward an Interpretive Theory of Culture") and 360–411 ("Person, Time, and Conduct in Bali").

1979
"From the Native's Point of View: On the Nature of Anthropological Understanding." In Paul Rabinow and William M. Sullivan, eds., *Interpretive Social Science: A Reader*. Berkeley: University of California Press. Pp. 225–241.

Georges, Robert A., and Michael O. Jones
1980
People Studying People: The Human Element in Fieldwork. Berkeley: University of California Press.

Glad, Betty
1966
Charles Evans Hughes and the Illusions of Innocence: A Study in American Diplomacy. Urbana: University of Illinois Press.

1969

"The Significance of Personality for Role Performance as Chairman of the Senate Foreign Relations Committee: A Comparison of Borah and Fulbright." Paper presented at the annual meeting of American Political Science Association, New York.

1973

"Contributions of Psychobiography." In Jeanne N. Knutson (ed.), *Handbook of Political Psychology*. San Francisco: Jossey-Bass. Pp. 296–321.

Gladwin, Thomas, and Seymour B. Sarason
1953
Truk: Man in Paradise. Viking Fund Publications in Anthropology, No. 20. New York: Wenner-Gren Foundation for Anthropological Research.

Glasse, Robert
1959
"Revenge and Redress among the Huli: A Preliminary Account." *Mankind* 5:273–289.

Gluck, Sherna
1979
"What's So Special About Women? Women's Oral History." *Frontiers* 2(2):3–14.

Goffman, Erving
1963
Stigma: Notes on the Management of Spoiled Identity. Englewood Cliffs, N.J.: Prentice-Hall.

Goldstein, Michael J., and James O. Palmer
1963
The Experience of Anxiety. New York: Oxford University Press.

Gollock, Georgina Anne
1928
Lives of Eminent Africans. New York: Longmans.

Gorden, Raymond L.
1956
"Dimensions of the Depth Interview." *American Journal of Sociology* 62:158–164.

Gordimer, Nadine
1979
Burger's Daughter. New York: Viking Press.

Gorer, Geoffrey
1938
Himalayan Village: An Account of the Lepchas of Sikkim. London: Michael Joseph, Ltd.

Gottschalk, Louis
1945
"The Historian and the Historical Document." In Louis Gottschalk et al., 1945, pp. 3–75.

Gottschalk, Louis, Clyde Kluckhohn, and Robert Angell (Eds.)
1945
The Use of Personal Documents in History, Anthropology, and Sociology. New York: Social Science Research Council, Bulletin 53.

Gough, Kathleen
1968
"Anthropology and Imperialism." *Monthly Review* 19(11):12–27.

Gregory, Dick
1964
Nigger: An Autobiography. New York: Dutton.

Grinnell, George Bird
1920
When Buffalo Ran. New Haven: Yale University Press.

Gronewold, Sylvia
1972
"Did Frank Hamilton Cushing Go Native?" In S.T. Kimball and James B. Watson (eds.), *Crossing Cultural Boundaries: The Anthropological Experience.* San Francisco: Chandler. Pp. 33–50.

Grönoset, Dagfinn
1975
Anna. Trans. from the Norwegian by Ingrid B. Josephson. New York: Knopf.

Halacy, D.J., Jr
1970
Man and Memory. New York: Harper and Row.

Haley, Alex
1966
(Ed.) *The Autobiography of Malcolm X.* With the Assistance of Alex Haley. New York: Grove Press. (Original 1964.)

1976
Roots. Garden City, N.Y.: Doubleday.

Hallowell, Alfred I.
1955
"The Self and Its Behavioral Environment." In *Culture and Experience.* Philadelphia: University of Pennsylvania Press. Pp. 75–110.

Harrell-Bond, Barbara
1976
"Studying Elites: Some Special Problems." In Rynkiewich and Spradley, 1976. Pp. 110–122.

Harrington, M.R.
1933
"The Life of a Lenape Boy." *Pennsylvania Archaeologist* 3:3–8.

Hatt, E. Demant
1931
Turi's Book of Lappland. London: Jonathan Cape. New York: Harper.

Hebard, Grace Raymond
1933
Sacajawea, a guide and interpreter of the Lewis and Clark expedition with an account of the travels of Toussaint Charbonneau, and of Jean Baptiste, the expedition papoose. Glendale, California: The Arthur H. Clark Co.

Heidegger, Martin
1962
Being and Time. Trans. John Macquarrie and Edward Robinson. New York: Harper.

Heider, Karl
1976
Ethnographic Film. Austin: University of Texas Press.

Henderson, James D., and Linda Roddy Henderson
1978
"Tania." In their *Ten Notable Women of Latin America.* Chicago: Nelson-Hall. Pp. 213–240.

Henry, Francis, and S. Saberwal (Eds.)
1969
Stress and Response in Fieldwork. New York: Holt.

Henry, Jules
1940
"A Method for Learning to Talk Primitive Languages." *American Anthropologist* 42:635–641.

Heschel, Abraham J.
1965
Who Is Man? Stanford, California: Stanford University Press.

Hill, W.W.
1935
"The Status of the Hermaphrodite and Transvestite in Navaho Culture." *American Anthropologist* 37:273–279.

Hockings, Paul (Ed.)
1975
Principles of Visual Anthropology. The Hague: Mouton & Co.

Hodge, Frederick Webb (Ed.)
1907
Handbook of the American Indians North of Mexico. Washington, D.C.: Smithsonian Institution. Bureau of American Ethnology, Bulletin 30.

Holmberg, Alan R.
1950
Nomads of the Long Bow: The Sirionó of Eastern Bolivia. Publications of the Institute of Social Anthropology No. 10. Washington, D.C.: Government Printing Office.

Holmes, T.H., and R.H. Rahe
1967
"The Social Readjustment Rating Scale." *Journal of Psychosomatic Research* 11(2): 213–218.

Holmes, T.H., and R.H. Rahe
1973
"Life Change and Illness Susceptibility." In John P. Scott and Edward Senay (eds.), *Separation and Depression: Clinical and Research Aspects.* Washington D.C.: American Association for the Advancement of Science, No. 94.

Honigmann, John J.
1976
"The Personal Approach in Cultural Anthropological Research." *Current Anthropology* 17(2):243–261.

Hook, Sidney
1943
The Hero in History. New York: John Day.

Howard, Helen A.
1941
War Chief Joseph. Caldwell, Idaho: Caxton.

Howard, Oliver O.
1881
Nez Perce Joseph, An Account of His Ancestors, His Lands, His Confederates, His Enemies, His Murders, His War, His Pursuit and Capture. Boston: Lee & Shepard.

Howell, Joseph T.
1973
Hard Living on Clay Street: Portraits of Blue Collar Families. New York: Anchor.

Hubbard, John Niles
1886
An Account of Sa-Go-Ye-Wat-Ha, or Red Jacket and His People. Albany.

Hughes, Charles C. (Ed.)
1974
Eskimo Boyhood: An Autobiography in Psychosocial Perspective. Lexington: University Press of Kentucky.

Hughes, Everett C.
1937
"Institutional Office and the Person." *American Journal of Sociology* 43:404–413.

Hyman, H.
1951
"Interviewing as a Scientific Procedure." In D. Lerner and H.D. Lasswell, eds., *The Policy Sciences: Recent Devleopments in Scope and Method.* Stanford, California: Stanford University Press. Pp. 203–216.

Indigena, Inc.
1974
Supysàua: A Documentary Report on the Conditions of Indian Peoples in Brazil. Berkeley, California: Indigena, News From Indian American and American Friends of Brazil.

Jackson, Donald (Ed.)
1955
Black Hawk: An Autobiography. Urbana: University of Illinois Press.

Jarvie, I.C.
1969
"The Problem of Ethical Integrity in Participant Observation." *Current Anthropology* 10(5):505–508.

Jelinek, Estelle C. (Ed.)
1980
Women's Autobiography: Essays in Criticism. Bloomington: Indiana University Press.

Johnson, Willis Fletcher
1891
The Red Record of the Sioux: Life of Sitting Bull and History of the Indian War of 1891.
Edgewood Publishing Co.

Jones, Ernest
1913
"The Case of Louis Bonaparte, King of Holland." *Journal of Abnormal Psychology*
8(5):289–301.

Jorgensen, Joseph G.
1971
"On Ethics and Anthropology." In Joseph G. Jorgensen and Richard N.
Adams, "Toward an Ethics for Anthropologists." *Current Anthropology* 12(3):
321–356.

Joyce, James
1922
Ulysses. Paris: Shakespeare and Co.

Kamano, Dennis K., and J.E. Drew
1961
"Selectivity in Memory of Personally Significant Material." *Journal of General
Psychology* 65:25–32.

Kaplan, B.
1961
"Cross-Cultural Use of Projective Techniques. In Francis L.K. Hsu, ed.,
Psychological Anthropology: Approaches to Culture and Personality. Homewood, Illinois:
Dorsey Press. Pp. 235–254.

Kardiner, Abram (with collaboration of Ralph Linton, Cora DuBois,
and James West)
1945
The Psychological Frontiers of Society. New York: Columbia University Press.

Kardiner, Abram, and Lionel Ovesey
1951
The Mark of Oppression: A Psychosocial Study of the American Negro. New York: Norton.

Kaufman, Sharon
1981
"Cultural Components of Identity in Old Age: A Case Study." *Ethos* 9(1):51–87.

Kelley, Jane Holden
1978
Yaqui Women: Contemporary Life Histories. Lincoln: University of Nebraska Press.

Kendall, Paul Murray
1965
The Art of Biography. New York: Norton.

Kennedy, John G.
1977
Struggle for Change in a Nubian Community: An Individual in Society and History. Palo Alto: Mayfield Publishing.

Kikumura, Akemi
1981
Through Harsh Winters: The Story of a Japanese Immigrant Woman. Novato, California: Chandler and Sharp.

Kingston, Maxine Hong
1976
The Woman Warrior: Memoirs of a Girlhood Among Ghosts. New York: Knopf.

Kloos, Peter
1969
"Role Conflicts in Social Fieldwork." *Current Anthropology* 10(5):509–523.

Kluckhohn, Clyde
1945
"The Personal Document in Anthropological Science." In Louis Gottschalk et al., 1945. Pp. 78–193.

Kluckhohn, C., H. Murray, and D. Schneider
1955
Personality in Nature, Society and Culture. New York: Knopf.

Kluckhohn, Florence
1940
"The Participant-Observer Technique in Small Communities." *American Journal of Sociology* 46:331–343.

Kocklars, Carl B.
1974
The Professional Fence. New York: Free Press.

1977
"Field Ethics for the Life History." In Robert S. Weppner, ed., *Street Ethnography: Selected Studies of Crime and Drug Use in Natural Settings.* Beverly Hills, California: Sage Publications. Pp. 201–226.

Koegel, Paul
1978
"Life History: A Vehicle Toward a Holistic Understanding of Deviance."
Unpublished manuscript.

Koppers, Wilhelm
1924
Unter Feuerland Indianern. Stuttgart: Strecker and Schröder.

1928
"Individualforschung unter den Primitiven." In *Besonderen unter den Yamana auf Feuerland.* Vienna: Schmidt-Festschrift (W. Koppers, ed.), Mechitharisten-Congregations. Pp. 349–365.

Kroeber, A.L.
1908
"Ethnology of the Gros Ventre." *Anthropological Papers of the American Museum of Natural History, War Experiences of Individuals* 1(4):196–222.

1953
(Ed.) *Anthropology Today.* Chicago: University of Chicago Press.

Kroeber, Theodora
1961
Ishi in Two Worlds: A Biography of the Last Wild Indian in North America. Berkeley: University of California Press.

Krueger, Starry
1973
The Whole Works: The Autobiography of a Young American Couple. New York: Random House.

Kuper, Hilda
1947a
An African Aristocracy: Rank among the Swazi. London: Oxford University Press.

1947b
The Uniform of Colour: A Study of White-Black Relationships in Swaziland. Johannesburg: University of Witwatersrand Press.

1963
The Swazi: A South African Kingdom. New York: Holt.

1965
Bite of Hunger: A Novel of Africa. New York: Harcourt.

1970
A Witch in My Heart: A Play about the Swazi People. London: Oxford University Press.

1978
Sobhuza II, Ngwenyama and King of Swaziland: The Story of an Hereditary Ruler and His Country. New York: Africana Publishing Company.

La Farge, Oliver
1929
Laughing Boy. Boston: Houghton Mifflin.

Laird, Carobeth
1979
Limbo. Novato, California: Chandler and Sharp.

Lame Deer, John (Fire), and Richard Erdoes
1972
Lame Deer: Seeker of Visions. New York: Simon and Schuster.

Landes, Ruth
1938
The Ojibwa Woman. New York: Columbia University Press.

Langness, L.L.
1965a
"Hysterical Psychosis in the New Guinea Highlands: A Bena Bena Example." *Psychiatry* 28:259–277.

1965b
The Life History in Anthropological Science. New York: Holt.

1970
"Entree into the Field: Highlands New Guinea." In Naroll and Cohen, 1970. Pp. 220–225.

1974
The Study of Culture. Novato, California: Chandler and Sharp.

1975
"Person, Role and Society." *Reviews in Anthropology* 2(2):281–285.

In press
"Individual Psychology and Culture Change: A Case from the Klallam." In Jay Miller and Carol Eastman, eds., *The Tsimshian and Their Neighbors: Essays in Honor of Viola Garfield.* Seattle: University of Washington Press.

Langness, L.L., and Gelya Frank
1978
"Fact, Fiction and the Ethnographic Novel." *Anthropology and Humanism Quarterly* 3(1 and 2):18–22.

Lasch, Christopher
1978
The Culture of Narcissism: American Life in an Age of Diminishing Expectations. New York: Norton.

Leighton, Alexander H., and Dorothea C. Leighton
1949
"Gregorio, The Hand-Trembler: A Psychobiological Personality Study of a Navaho Indian." *Papers of the Peabody Museum of American Archaeology and Ethnology*, Vol. XL. Cambridge, Mass.

Le Bar, Frank M.
1970
"Coding Ethnographic Materials." In Naroll and Cohen, 1970. Pp. 707–720. Pp. 707–720.

Lerner, D.
1956
"Interviewing Frenchmen." *American Journal of Sociology* 62:187–194.

Levinson, D.J., C.M. Darrow, E.B. Klein, M.H. Levinson, and B. McKee
1974
"The Psychosocial Development of Men in Eariy Adulthood and the Mid-Life Transition." In D.F. Ricks, H. Thomas, and M. Roff, eds., *Life History Research in Psychopathology*, Vol. 3. Minneapolis: University of Minnesota Press.

Levy, Robert I.
1973
Tahitians: Mind and Experience in the Society Islands. Chicago: University of Chicago Press.

Lewis, Oscar
1959
Five Families: Mexican Case Studies in the Culture of Poverty. New York: Basic Books.

1961
The Children of Sánchez: Autobiography of a Mexican Family. New York: Random House.

1964
Pedro Martinez: A Mexican Peasant and His Family. New York: Random House.

1965
La Vida: A Puerto Rican Family in the Culture of Poverty—San Juan and New York. New York: Vintage Books.

Lewis, Oscar, Ruth M. Lewis, and Susan M. Rigdon
1977a
Four Men. Urbana: University of Illinois Press.

1977b
Four Women. Urbana: University of Illinois Press.

1978
Neighbors. Urbana: University of Illinois Press.

Lincecum, Gideon
1906
Life of Apushimata. Mississippi Historical Society Publication 9, pp. 115–485.

Linde, Charlotte
1978
"The Creation of Coherence in Life Stories." Manuscript to appear. Norwood, N.J.: Ablex Corp.

1980
"The Life Story: A Temporally Discontinuous Discourse Type." Paper presented at the Kassel Workshop on Psycholinguistic Models of Production, Kassel, W. Germany, H.W. Dechert, ed.

Linderman, Frank B.
1930
America: the Life Story of a Great Indian, Plenty-Coups, Chief of the Crows. New York: John Day Co.

1932
Red Mother. New York: John Day Co.

Link, H.C.
1943
"An Experiment in Depth Interviewing." *Public Opinion Quarterly* (7)2:267–279.

Love, W. DeLoss
1900
Samson Occum and the Christian Indians of New England. Boston: Pilgrim Press.

Lowe, Martha Perry
1881
The Story of Chief Joseph. Boston: D. Lothrop & Co.

Lowie, Robert H.
1935
The Crow Indians. New York: Farrar & Rinehart.

1940
"Native Languages as Ethnographic Tools." *American Anthropologist* 42:81–89.

Lurie, Nancy Oestreich
1961
Mountain Wolf Woman, Sister of Crashing Thunder: The Autobiography of a Winnebago Woman. Ann Arbor: University of Michigan Press.

Maccoby, Eleanor, and N. Maccoby
1954
"The Interview: A Tool of Social Science." In G. Lindzey, ed., *Handbook of Social Psychology.* Cambridge, Mass.: Addison-Wesley. Pp. 449–487.

McFadden, Mary
1975
Odysseus Succeeds: The Life History of John Cookthanasis. Ph.D. dissertation, Department of Anthropology, Washington State University, Pullman, Washington.

McKenny, Thomas L., and James Hall
1933
The Indian Tribes of North America, with Biographical Sketches and Anecdotes of the Principal Chiefs. New edition, edited by Frederick Webb Hodge. 3 vols. Edinburgh: John Grant. (Original 1836.)

McWhorter, Lucullus Virgil
1940
Yellow Wolf, His Own Story. Caldwell, Idaho: Caxton.

Malinowski, Bronislaw
1922
Argonauts of the Western Pacific. New York: Dutton.

Mandelbaum, David G.
1973
"The Study of Life History: Gandhi." *Current Anthropology* 14(3):177–206.

Marriott, Alice
1948
Maria: The Potter of San Ildefonso. Norman: University of Oklahoma Press.

Maurois, André
1929
Aspects of Biography. S.C. Roberts, trans. Cambridge: The University Press.

Mauss, Marcel
1938
"Une catégorie de l'esprit humain: la notion de personne celle de 'moi.' "
Journal of the Royal Anthropological Institute 68:63–281.

Mazlish, Bruce
1972
In Search of Nixon: A Psychohistorical Inquiry. New York: Basic Books.

Mead, Margaret
1933
"More Comprehensive Field Methods." *American Anthropologist* 35(1):1–15.

1939
"Native Languages as Field Work Tools." *American Anthropologist* 41:189–206.

1953
"National Character." In A.L. Kroeber, ed., 1953. Pp. 642–667.

1958
Preface. In Carstairs, *The Twice-Born.*

1969
"Research with Human Beings: A Model Derived from Anthropological Field
Practice." *Daedalus* 98:361–386.

1970
"The Art and Technology of Fieldwork." In Naroll and Cohen, 1970. Pp. 246–
265.

1975
Blackberry Winter: My Earlier Years. New York: Pocket Books. (Original 1972.)

Merton, Robert K., Marjorie Fiske, and Patricia L. Kendall
1956
The Focused Interview. Glencoe, Illinois: Free Press.

Meyerhoff, Hans
1960
Time in Literature. Berkeley: University of California Press. (Original 1955.)

Michelson, Truman
1925
The Autobiography of a Fox Indian Woman. Bureau of American Ethnology, Fortieth Annual Report. Washington, D.C.: Smithsonian Institution.

1932
The Narrative of a Southern Cheyenne Woman. Washington, D.C.: Smithsonian Miscellaneous Collections, vol. 87 no. 5.

1933
"Narrative of an Arapaho Woman." *American Anthropologist* 35:595–610.

Mihalic, Francis
1971
The Jacaranda Dictionary and Grammar of Melanesian Pidgin. Port Moresby, Papua New Guinea: Jacaranda Press.

Mintz, Sidney W.
1960, 1974
Worker in the Cane: A Puerto Rican Life History. New Haven: Yale University Press, 1960. New York: Norton, 1974.

1979
"The Anthropological Interview and the Life History." *Oral History Review.* Pp. 18–26.

Misch, Georg
1973
A History of Autobiography in Antiquity. E.W. Dickes, trans. Westport, Conn.: Greenwood Press.

Moerman, Michael
1974
"Accomplishing Ethnicity." In Roy Turner, ed., *Ethnomethodology.* Harmondsworth, Middlesex, England: Penguin Books. Pp. 54–68.

Momaday, Navarre Scott
1976
The Names: A Memoir by N. Scott Momaday. New York: Harper.

Moore, Alexander G.
1973
Life Cycles in Atchalán: The Diverse Careers of Certain Guatemalans. New York: Teachers College Press.

Mullett, Charles F.
1963
Biography as History: Men and Movements in Europe since 1500. (Publication No. 49, Service Center for Teachers of History.) New York: Macmillan.

Murdock, George Peter, et al.
1971
Outline of Cultural Materials. New Haven: Human Relations Area Files.

Murphy, John J.
1959
The Book of Pidgin English. Brisbane, Queensland, Australia: W.R. Smith & Patterson Pty. Ltd.

Murphy, Robert F.
1964
"Social Distance and the Veil." *American Anthropologist* 66(6)(Part 2):1257–1274.

Murray, Henry A.
1938
Explorations in Personality. New York: Oxford University Press.

Myerhoff, Barbara G.
1978
Number Our Days. New York: Dutton.

1979
"Life History Among the Elderly: Performance, Visibility, and Re-membering." Manuscript.

1980a
"Re-membered Lives." *Parabola: Myth and the Quest for Meaning* 5(1)(February):74–77.

1980b
"Telling One's Story." *The Center Magazine* 13(2):22–40.

Myerhoff, Barbara, and Andrei Simić (Eds.)
1978
Life's Career—Aging: Cultural Variations on Growing Old. Beverly Hills, California: Sage Publications.

Myerhoff, Barbara, and Virginia Tufte
1975
"Life History as Integration: An Essay on an Experiential Model." *Gerontologist* December 541–544.

Myers, Fred R.
1979
"Emotions and the Self: A Theory of Personhood and Political Order among Pintupi Aborigines." *Ethos* 7(4)(Winter):343–370.

Nabokov, Peter
1967
Two Leggings: The Making of a Crow Warrior. New York: Thomas Y. Crowell.

Nadel, Siegfried F.
1939
"The Interview Technique in Social Anthropology." In F.C. Bartlett, ed., *The Study of Society.* New York: Macmillan. Pp. 317–327.

Nagourney, Peter
1978
"The Basic Assumptions of Literary Biography." *Biography* 1(2):86–104.

Naroll, Raoul, and Ronald Cohen (Eds.)
1970
A Handbook of Method in Cultural Anthropology. Garden City, N.Y.: Natural History Press.

Nash, Alanna
1978
Dolly! Los Angeles: Reed Books.

1979
"Goodbye Dolly!" *Writer's Digest.* July:18–24.

Nash, Dennison, and Ronald Wintrob
1972
"The Emergence of Self-Consciousness in Ethnography." *Current Anthropology* 13:527–542.

Neihardt, John G.
1932
Black Elk Speaks, Being a Life Story of a Holy Man of the Oglala Sioux. New York: William Morrow.

1970
When the Tree Flowered. An Authentic Tale of the Old Sioux World. The Fictional Autobiography of Eagle Voice, A Sioux Indian. Lincoln: University of Nebraska Press. New York: Macmillan, 1951.

Ntara, Samuel Yosia
1934
Man of Africa. London: Religious Tract Society.

Nuligak
1966
I, Nuligak. Maurice Metayer, trans. Toronto: Peter Martin Associates.

O'Beirne, Harry F.
1891
Leaders and Leading Men of the Indian Territory with Interesting Biographical Sketches.
Chicago: American Publishers Association.

Obeyesekere, Gananath
1977
"Psychocultural Exegesis of a Case of Spirit Possession in Sri Lanka." In
Crapanzano and Garrison, 1977. Pp. 235–294.

Okada, John
1976
No-No Boy. San Francisco: Combined Asian American Resources Project, Inc.

Okimoto, Daniel
1971
American in Disguise. New York: Walker/Weatherhill.

Olney, James
1972
Metaphors of Self: The Meaning of Autobiography. Princeton: Princeton University
Press.

1980
Autobiography: Essays Theoretical and Critical. Princeton: Princeton University Press.

Opler, Morris E.
1938a
"A Chiricahua Apache's Account of the Geronimo Campaign of 1886." *New
Mexico Historical Review* 13:360–386.

1938b
"Dirty Boy: A Jicarilla Tale of Raid and War." *American Anthropological Association Memoirs* 52.

1941
An Apache Life-way. Chicago: University of Chicago Press.

1969
Apache Odyssey: A Journey between Two Worlds. New York: Holt.

Oskison, John M.
1938
Tecumseh and His Times. The Story of a Great Indian. New York: Putnam.

Paddock, John
1965a
"A Review of *Five Families* and *The Children of Sánchez.*" In *MesoAmerican Notes 6,*
pp. 37–50. Department of Anthropology, University of the Americas, Mexico
City.

1965b
"Private Lives and Anthropological Publications." In *MesoAmerican Notes 6,*
pp. 59–68. Department of Anthropology, University of the Americas, Mexico
City.

1965c
"Appendix: *The Children of Sánchez* in the Headlines." In *MesoAmerican Notes 6,*
pp. 69–140. Department of Anthropology, University of the Americas, Mexico
City.

Panel on Privacy and Behavioral Research
1967
Privacy and Behavioral Research. Washington, D.C.: Executive Office of the
President, Office of Science and Technology.

Parsons, Elsie Clews
1919
"Waiyautitea of Zuni, New Mexico." *Scientific Monthly* 9:443–457.

1921
"A Narrative of the Ten'a of Anvik, Alaska." *Anthropos* 16:51–71.

1922 (Ed.)
American Indian Life. New York: B.W. Huebsch.

Parssinen, Carol Ann
1974
"In Pursuit of Ethnography: The Seduction of Science by Art." University of
Pennsylvania, Center for Urban Ethnography. Manuscript.

1975
"Paradigms of Ethnographic Realism." Selected Proceedings of the 1975
Conference on Culture and Communication. Working Papers in Culture and

Communication 1:1. Philadelphia: Department of Anthropology, Temple University. Pp. 98–107.

Pascal, Roy
1960
Design and Truth in Autobiography. London: Routledge.

Passin, Herbert
1942
"Tarahumara Prevarication: A Problem in Field Method." *American Anthropologist* 44:235–247.

Patterson, John Barton (Ed.)
1882
Autobiography of Ma-Ka-Tai-Me-She-Kia-Kiak, or Black Hawk. St. Louis: Continental Printing Co.

Paul, Benjamin
1953
"Interview Techniques and Field Relationships." In A.L. Kroeber, ed., 1953. Pp. 430–451.

Pearsall, Marion
1970
"Participant Observation as Role and Method in Behavioral Research." In William J. Filstead, ed., 1970. Pp. 340–352.

Perham, Margery F. (Ed.)
1936
Ten Africans. London: Faber & Faber.

Pilisuk, Marc, and Phyllis Pilisuk (Eds.)
1971
Poor Americans: How the White Poor Live. Chicago: Aldine.

Polking, Kirk, and Leonard S. Meranus (Eds.)
1978
Law and the Writer. Cincinnati: Writer's Digest.

Porter, Roger J., and H.R. Wolf
1973
The Voice Within: Reading and Writing Autobiography. New York: Knopf.

Powdermaker, Hortense
1966
Stranger and Friend: The Way of an Anthropologist. New York: Norton.

Pozas, Ricardo
1962
Juan the Chamula: An Ethnological Re-Creation of the Life of a Mexican Indian. Berkeley: University of California Press.

Preston, Caroline
1964
"Psychological Testing with Northwest Coast Alaskan Eskimos." *Genetic Psychology Monographs* 69:323–419.

Rabinow, Paul
1977
Reflections on Fieldwork in Morocco. Berkeley: University of California Press.

Radin, Paul
1913
"Personal Reminiscences of a Winnebago Indian." *Journal of American Folklore* 26:293–318.

1920
The Autobiography of a Winnebago Indian. University of California Publications in American Archaeology and Ethnology, vol. 16, no. 7, pp. 381–473.

1926
(Ed.) *Crashing Thunder, The Autobiography of an American Indian.* New York: Appleton.

1927a
The Story of the American Indian. New York: Boni and Liveright.

1927b
Primitive Man as Philosopher. New York: Appleton.

1933
The Method and Theory of Ethnology: An Essay in Criticism. London: McGraw-Hill.

Ramos, Alcida R., and Kenneth L. Taylor
1979
Yąnomamö: The Long Struggle for a Demarcated Territory. *Anthropology Resource Center Newsletter* 3(4)(December):2.

Randall, Margaret
1974
Cuban Women Now: Interviews with Cuban Women. Toronto, Canada: The Women's Press and Dumont Press.

Rapaport, David
1961
Emotions and Memory. The Menninger Clinic Monograph Series, No. 2. New York: Science Editions.

Rasmussen, Knud
1908
The People of the Polar North: A Record. London: Kegan Paul.

Read, Kenneth E.
1965
The High Valley. New York: Scribners.

1980
Other Voices: The Style of a Male Homosexual Tavern. Novato, California: Chandler and Sharp.

Reckless, Walter C., and L.S. Selling
1937
"A Sociological and Psychiatric Interview Compared." *American Journal of Orthopsychiatry* 7:532–539.

Redfield, Robert, and Alfonso Villa Rojas
1934
"A Village Leader: A Native Autobiography." In *Chan Kom*, Publication No. 448 of the Carnegie Institution of Washington. Pp. 212–230.

Reichard, Gladys
1934
Spider Woman: A Story of Navaho Weavers and Chanters. New York: Macmillan.

1939
Dezba: Woman of the Desert. New York: J.J. Augustin.

Reyher, Rebecca Hourwich
1948
Zulu Woman. New York: Columbia University Press.

Reynolds, Vernon
1976
The Biology of Human Action. San Francisco: W.H. Freeman.

Rich, Adrienne
1978
"Phantasia for Elvira Shatayev." In her *The Dream of a Common Language: Poems 1974–1977.* New York: Norton. Pp. 4–6.

Richards, A.I.
1939
"The Development of Field Work Methods in Social Anthropology." In *The Study of Society*. F.C. Bartlett (ed.) New York: Macmillan. Pp. 272–316.

Richardson, Miles
1975
"Anthropologist—The Myth Teller." *American Ethnologist* 2:517–533.

Richardson, Stephen A., Barbara Snell Dohrenwend, and David Klein
1965
Interviewing: Its Forms and Functions. New York: Basic Books.

Riegel, Klaus F.
1974
"Adult Life Crises: A Dialectic Interpretation of Development." In N. Datan and L.H. Ginsberg (eds.), *Life-Span Developmental Psychology: Normative Life Crises*. New York: Academic Press.

Riesman, Paul
1977
Freedom in Fulani Social Life: An Introspective Ethnography. Chicago: University of Chicago Press.

Rivers, W.H.R.
1910
"The Genealogical Method of Anthropological Inquiry." *Sociological Review* 3:1–12.

Rogers, Carl R.
1945
"The Non-directive Method as a Technique for Social Research." *American Journal of Sociology* 50:279–283.

Rohner, Ronald P. (Ed.)
1969
The Ethnography of Franz Boas: Letters and Diaries of Franz Boas Written on the Northwest Coast from 1886 to 1931. Chicago: University of Chicago Press.

Rosaldo, Michelle Z.
1980
Knowledge and Passion: Ilongot Notions of Self and Social Life. Cambridge, England: Cambridge University Press.

Rosaldo, Renato
1976
"The Story of Tukbaw: 'They Listen as He Orates.' " In F. Reynolds and D. Capps, *The Biographical Process: Studies in the History and Psychology of Religion.* The Hague: Mouton & Co. Pp. 121–151.

Rosengarten, Theodore
1975
All God's Dangers: The Life of Nate Shaw. New York: Avon Books.

Rousseau, Jean-Jacques
1954
The Confessions. J.M. Cohen, trans. Harmondsworth, Middlesex, England: Penguin Books. (Completed 1765; first published 1781.)

Roy, Manisha
1975
Bengali Women. Chicago: University of Chicago Press.

Royal Anthropological Institute of Great Britain and Ireland
1954
Notes and Queries on Anthropology. London: Routledge & Kegan Paul.

Ruby, Jay
1977
"The Image Mirrored: Reflexivity and the Documentary Film." *Journal of the University Film Association,* 24(1):3–11.

Rush, Florence
1977
"The Freudian Cover-up: The Sexual Abuse of Children." *Chrysalis* 1(1):31–45.

Rynkiewich, Michael A., and James P. Spradley
1976
Ethics and Anthropology: Dilemmas in Fieldwork. New York: Wiley.

Sachs, Wulf
1937
Black Hamlet, The Mind of an African Negro Revealed by Psychoanalysis. London: Geoffrey Books.

Sapir, Edward
1921
"The Life of a Nootka Indian." *Queens Quarterly* 28:232–243; 351–367. (Reprinted in Parsons 1922.)

Sartre, Jean-Paul
1963
Saint Genet: Actor and Martyr. Bernard Frechtman, trans. New York: George Braziller. (Original 1952.)

1966a
The Words. Trans. Bernard Frechtman. Greenwich, Connecticut: Fawcett. (Original 1964.)

1966b
Being and Nothingness: An Essay on Phenomenological Ontology. Trans. Hazel E. Barnes. New York: Washington Square Press. (Original 1943.)

Savage, Willam W., Jr. (Ed.)
1977
Indian Life: Transforming an American Myth. Norman: University of Oklahoma Press.

Schapera, I.
1935
"Field Methods in the Study of Modern Culture Contacts." *Africa* 8:315–328.

Scheff, Thomas J.
1977
"The Distancing of Emotion in Ritual." *Current Anthropology* 18(3)(September):483–505.

1979
Catharsis in Healing, Ritual, and Drama. Berkeley: University of California Press.

Schmidt, W.
1906
"Die Moderne Ethnologie." *Anthropos I*:134–163; 318–387; 592–643; 950–997.

Scholte, Bob
1970
"Toward a Self-Reflexive Anthropology." *Critical Anthropology* 1(2):3–33.

Schwartz, Norman B.
1977
A Milpero of Peten, Guatemala: Autobiography and Cultural Analysis. Newark, Delaware: University of Delaware Latin American Studies Program, Occasional Papers and Monographs, No. 2.

Scott, Lalla
1966
Karnee: A Paiute Narrative, the Story of Annie Lowry. Reno: University of Nevada Press.

Seiler, Michael
1980
"Sailor, 18, Found Guilty in Sex Case." *Los Angeles Times.* Sec. 1, p. 1, Aug. 19.

Shaw, Bruce
1980
"Life History Writing in Anthropology: A Methodological Review." *Mankind* 12(3):226–233.

Shaw, Clifford R.
1930
The Jack-Roller: A Delinquent Boy's Own Story. Chicago: University of Chicago Press.

Shirer, William L.
1960
The Rise and Fall of the Third Reich. New York: Simon & Schuster.

Shweder, Richard A.
1979
"Rethinking Culture and Personality Theory, Part I: A Critical Examination of Two Classical Postulates." *Ethos* 7(3):255–278.

Simmel, Georg
1950
The Sociology of Georg Simmel. Trans. K.H. Wolff. Glencoe, Ill.: Free Press.

Simmons, Leo W.
1942
Sun Chief: The Autobiography of a Hopi Indian. New Haven: Yale University Press.

Sjoberg, Gideon (Ed.)
1971
Ethics, Politics, and Social Research. Cambridge, Mass.: Schenkman.

Smith, M.F.
1954
Baba of Karo. London: Faber & Faber.

Sone, Monica
1953
Nisei Daughter. Boston: Little, Brown.

Spain, David
1972
"On the Use of Projective Tests for Research in Psychological Anthropology." In Francis L.K. Hsu, ed., *Psychological Anthropology*, rev. ed. Cambridge, Mass.: Schenkman. Pp. 276–308.

Spiegel, Claire
1980
"2nd Sailor Guilty of Lesbian Acts." *Los Angeles Times*, Section 1, Page 1, August 21.

Spiegel, John P.
1959
"Some Cultural Aspects of Transference and Countertransference." In J.H. Masserman, ed., *Science and Psychoanalysis: Individual and Family Dynamics*, vol. 2. New York: Grune & Stratton. Pp. 160–182.

Spiegelberg, Herbert
1972
Phenomenology in Psychology and Psychiatry. Evanston, Ill.: Northwestern University Press.

Spiro, Melford E.
1961
"Social Systems, Personality, and Functional Analysis." In *Studying Personality Cross-Culturally*, Bert Kaplan (ed.), Evanston, Illinois: Row, Peterson. Pp. 93–127.

1972
"An Overview and Suggested Reorientation." In Francis L.K. Hsu, ed., *Psychological Anthropology*, rev. ed. Cambridge, Mass.: Schenkman. Pp. 573–607.

Splawn, Andrew J.
1917
Ka-Mi-Akin, The Last Hero of the Yakimas. Caldwell, Idaho: Caxton. Portland, Oregon: Kilham.

Spradley, James P.
1969
Guests Never Leave Hungry: The Autobiography of James Sewid, a Kwakiutl Indian. New Haven: Yale University Press.

1979
The Ethnographic Interview. New York: Holt.

Standing Bear, Luther (Chief)
1928
My People the Sioux. Boston: Houghton Mifflin.

1933
Land of the Spotted Eagle. Boston: Houghton Mifflin.

Stanley, J.M.
1852
Portraits of North American Indians. Washington, D.C.: Smithsonian Institution.

Stanley, Julia P., and Susan J. Wolfe (Robbins)
1978
"Toward a Feminist Aesthetic." *Chrysalis* 6:57–71.

Starobinski, Jean
1971
"The Style of Autobiography." In S.B. Chatman, ed., *Literary Style, A Symposium.* New York: Oxford University Press. Pp. 285–296.

Stein, Gertrude
1933
The Autobiography of Alice B. Toklas. New York: Random House.

1934
The Making of Americans: The Hersland Family. New York: Harcourt.

1937
Everybody's Autobiography. New York: Random House.

Steir, Charles (Ed.)
1978
Blue Jolts: True Stories from the Cuckoo's Nest. Washington, D.C.: New Republic Books.

Steward, Julian
1938
Panatubiui, An Owens Valley Paiute. Washington, D.C.: Smithsonian Institution. Bureau of American Ethnology, Bulletin 119.

Stewart, Grace
1979
A New Mythos: The Novel of the Artist as Heroine 1877–1977. Monographs in Women's Studies. St. Alban's, Vermont: Eden Press.

Stocking, George W., Jr.
1968
"Franz Boas and the Culture Concept in Historical Perspective." In his *Race, Culture, and Evolution: Essays in the History of Anthropology.* Pp. 195–233. New York: Free Press.

Stone, William L.
1841
The Life and Times of Red Jacket or Sa-Go-Ye-Wat-Ha. New York: Wiley.

1842
Uncas and Miantonomoh. New York: Dayton and Newman.

1865
Life of Joseph Brant. 2 volumes. Albany: J. Munsell.

Strauss, A., and Schatzman, L.
1960
"Cross-class Interviewing: An Analysis of Interaction and Communicative Styles." In R.N. Adams and J.J. Preiss, eds., *Human Organization Research: Field Relations and Techniques.* Homewood, Illinois: Dorsey Press. Pp. 205–213.

Sullivan, Harry Stack
1954
The Psychiatric Interview. Helen Swick Perry and Mary Ladd Gawel, eds., New York: Norton.

Sundberg, Norman D.
1977
Assessment of Persons. Englewood Cliffs, N.J.: Prentice-Hall.

Thatcher, B.B.
1832
Indian Biography: Or, An Historical Account of Those Individuals Who Have Been Distinguished Among the North American Natives as Orators, Warriors, Statesmen and Other Remarkable Characters. New York: J. & J. Harper.

Thomas, William I., and Florian Znaniecki
1918–1920
The Polish Peasant in Europe and America. 5 volumes. Boston: Richard G. Badger.

Thoreau, Henry D.
1893
Walden: Or, Life in the Woods. Boston: Houghton Mifflin. (Original 1854.)

Tucker, Glenn
1956
Tecumseh: Vision of Glory. New York: Bobbs-Merrill.

Turki, Fawaz
1974
The Disinherited: Journal of a Palestinian Exile. New York: Monthly Review Press.

Turnbull, Colin
1961
The Forest People: A Study of the Pygmies of the Congo. New York: Simon and Schuster.

1972
The Mountain People. New York: Simon and Schuster.

Turner, Jim L.
1980
"Yes I am Human: Autobiography of a 'Retarded Career.' " *Journal of Community Psychology* 8:3–8.

Turner, Katherine C.
1951
Red Men Calling on the Great White Father. Norman: University of Oklahoma Press.

Turner, Victor
1957
Schism and Continuity in an African Society. Manchester: Rhodes-Livingston Institute.

Underhill, Ruth
1936
The Autobiography of a Papago Woman. Memoirs of the American Anthropological Association, No. 46. Menasha, Wisconsin: American Anthropological Association.

Valentine, Charles A.
1968
Culture and Poverty: Critique and Counter-Proposals. Chicago: University of Chicago Press.

Van den Berg, J.H.
1964
The Changing Nature of Man: Introduction to a Historical Psychology. New York: Dell.

Van Gennep, Arnold
1960
The Rites of Passage. Chicago: University of Chicago Press.

Vansina, Jan
1965
Oral Tradition, A Study in Historical Methodology. Chicago: Aldine.

Vestal, Stanley
1932
Sitting Bull: Champion of the Sioux. Boston: Houghton Mifflin.

1934
Warpath. The True Story of the Fighting Sioux, Told in a Biography of Chief White Bull. Boston: Houghton Mifflin.

Vidich, A., J. Bensman, R. Risley, R. Ries, and H.S. Becker
1958
"Comments on 'Freedom and Responsibility in Research.' " *Human Organization* 17(4):2–7.

Vischer, A.L.
1947
Old Age: Its Compensations and Rewards. New York: Macmillan. London: Allen and Unwin.

Wallis, Wilson D.
1919
Sun Dance of the Canadian Dakota. Anthropological Papers of the American Museum of Natural History, vol. 16, Personal Narratives. New York: The Trustees. Pp. 317–381.

Washburne, Heluiz Chandler
1940
Land of the Good Shadows. The Life Story of Anauta, An Eskimo Woman. New York: John Day Co.

Washington, Booker T.
1963
Up From Slavery: An Autobiography. New York: Bantam Books. (Original 1901.)

Watson, Lawrence C.
1976
"Understanding a Life History as a Subjective Document: Hermeneutical and Phenomenological Perspectives." *Ethos* 4:95–131.

1978
"The Study of Personality and the Study of Individuals: Two Approaches, Two Types of Explanation." *Ethos* 6(1):3–21.

Watson, Virginia
1916
The Princess Pocahontas. Philadelphia: Penn Publishing Co.

Wax, Murray L., and Joan Cassell (Eds.)
1979
Federal Regulations: Ethical Issues and Social Research. American Association for the Advancement of Science. Selected Symposium Series. No. 36. Boulder, Colorado: Westview Press.

Wax, Rosalie H.
1971
Doing Fieldwork: Warnings and Advice. Chicago: University of Chicago Press.

Wedge, Bryant
1968
"Khrushchev at a Distance: A Study of Public Personality," *Trans-Action* 5:24–28, 6:63–64.

Welch, Andrew
1841
A Narrative of the Early Days and Remembrances of Oceola Nikkanochee; Prince of Econchatti, a Young Seminole Indian; Son of Econchatti-Mico, King of the Red Hills, in Florida. Written by his guardian. London: Hatchard and Son.

Wells, H.G.
1934
Experiment in Autobiography: Discoveries and Conclusions of a Very Ordinary Brain (Since 1886). New York: Macmillan.

White, Leslie
1943
"Autobiography of an Acoma Indian." In *New Material From Acoma.* Washington, D.C.: Smithsonian Institution. Bureau of American Ethnology, Bulletin 136. Pp. 326–337.

White, Robert W.
1952
Lives in Progress: A Study of the Natural Growth of Personality. New York: Holt.

1964
(**Ed.**) *The Study of Lives: Essays on Personality in Honor of Henry A. Murray.* New York: Atherton.

Whitman, Walt
1855
Leaves of Grass. Brooklyn, N.Y. Privately published.

Whittemore, R., P. Koegel, and L.L. Langness
1980
"The Life History Approach to Mental Retardation." Working Paper No. 12, Socio-Behavioral Research Group, Mental Retardation Research Center, University of California, Los Angeles.

Wilkie, James W.
1967
"Postulates of the Oral History Center for Latin America." *Journal of Library History*, 2(1):45–55.

Williams, F.E.
1939
"The Reminiscences of Ahuia Ova." *Journal of the Royal Anthropological Institute* 69:11–44.

Wilson, Gilbert L.
1917
Agriculture of the Hidatsa Indians. An Indian Interpretation. Minneapolis: University of Minnesota, Studies in the Social Sciences, No. 9.

1924
"The Horse and the Dog in Hidatsa Culture." New York: American Museum Press. *Anthropological Papers of the American Museum of Natural History,* vol. 15, part 2, pp. 125–311.

1928
"Hidatsa Eagle Trapping." New York: American Museum Press. *Anthropological Papers of the American Museum of Natural History,* vol. 30, part 4, pp. 99–246.

n.d.
Goodbird the Indian, His Story. New York: Revell.

Wilson, Peter J.
1975
Oscar: An Inquiry into the Nature of Sanity. New York: Vintage Books.

Winter, Edward H.
1965
Beyond the Mountains of the Moon: The Lives of Four Africans. Urbana: University of Illinois Press.

Wolfensberger, W.
1972
The Principle of Normalization in Human Services. Toronto: National Institute on Mental Retardation.

Wolfenstein, E. Victor
1967
The Revolutionary Personality: Lenin, Trotsky, Gandhi. Princeton: Princeton University Press.

Wong, Jade Snow
1950
Fifth Chinese Daughter. New York: Harper & Row.

Wood, Norman B.
1906
Lives of Famous Indian Chiefs. Chicago: L.W. Walter Co. Aurora, Ill.: American Indian Historical Publishing Co.

Woodward, Kenneth L., with Scott Sullivan
1980
Jean-Paul Sartre, 1905–1980." *Newsweek,* April 28, p. 77.

Wrye, Harriet, and Jacqueline Churilla
1979
"Looking Inward, Looking Backward: Reminiscence and the Life Review." *Frontiers: A Journal of Women Studies* II (2):77–84.

X, Malcolm
1966
The Autobiography of Malcolm X. With the assistance of Alex Haley. New York: Grove Press.

Yoshida, Jim
1972
The Two Worlds of Jim Yoshida. With Bill Hosokawa. New York: William Morrow.

Zimmerman, Charles L.
1941
White Eagle: Chief of the Poncas. Harrisburg, Penn.: Telegraph Press.

Index